SOCIO-HISTORICAL EXAMINATION OF RELIGION AND MINISTRY: A JOURNAL OF THE FAITHX PROJECT

SHERM

VOLUME 1, NO. 1
SPRING 2019

www.shermjournal.org

ISSN 2637-7519 (print)
ISSN 2637-7500 (online)
ISBN 978-1-5326-8495-1

Wipf and Stock Publishers
199 West 8th Avenue, Suite 3
Eugene, OR 97401-2960
Tel: (541) 344-1528

Printed copies of this issue are available for purchase from Wipf and Stock Publishers through their website www.wipfandstock.com or by email orders@wipfandstock.com.

General Editor:
Darren M. Slade, Ph.D.

Editorial Advisory Board:
Abimbola A. Adelakun, Ph.D.
Peter Antoci, Ph.D.
Robert Gregory Cavin, Ph.D.
Mike Clawson, Ph.D.
Carlos Colombetti, Ph.D.
Evan Fales, Ph.D.
Anthony Gill, Ph.D.
Ken Howard, M.Div., M.Ed.
Mark A. Moore, Ph.D.
Josh Packard, Ph.D.
Amy Beth Rell, Ph.D.
Robert R. Stains, Jr., M.Ed.

Socio-Historical Examination of Religion and Ministry (SHERM journal) is a biannual, not-for-profit, free peer-reviewed academic journal that publishes the latest social-scientific, historiographic, and ecclesiastic research on religious institutions and their ministerial practices. SHERM is dedicated to the critical and scholarly inquiry of historical and contemporary religious phenomena, both from within particular religious traditions and across cultural boundaries, so as to inform the broader socio-historical analysis of religion and its related fields of study.

The purpose of SHERM is to provide a scholarly medium for the social-scientific study of religion where specialists can publish advanced studies on religious trends, theologies, rituals, philosophies, socio-political influences, or experimental and applied ministry research in the hopes of generating enthusiasm for the vocational and academic study of religion while fostering collegiality among religious specialists. Its mission is to provide academics, professionals, and nonspecialists with critical reflections and evidence-based insights into the socio-historical study of religion and, where appropriate, its implications for ministry and expressions of religiosity.

Editorial Advisory Board

SHERM journal is a division of the non-profit organization, FaithX Project (a religiously affiliated institute), and therefore, receives endowments from FaithX to maintain a significant presence within academia and the broader faith community. Nonetheless, the journal is overseen by an independent, religiously unaffiliated Editorial Advisory Board to ensure the content of the published articles meet stringent standards of critical scholarship uninfluenced by theological or ideological allegiances.

Copyright Privileges

When publishing an article through SHERM, authors are able to retain copyright privileges over their research. As part of the rights agreement, however, all authors wishing to publish their research through SHERM must transfer exclusive licensing rights over to SHERM, thereby granting SHERM the right to claim the article as part of its publishing proprietary corpus. In other words, authors retain copyright credit for the article but SHERM becomes the sole publisher of the material. Nonetheless, SHERM is a non-restrictive licensing publication, which means authors (as copyright owners of their research) are allowed to share and repost their article on any website of their choosing.

This transfer of exclusive licensing rights does not mean authors forfeit their copyright privileges. As partners with SHERM, upon acceptance and publication of an article, authors are automatically granted the right to share, disseminate, use, and repost their article in any way they deem necessary to expand the visibility of their publication. Likewise, authors retain all intellectual property rights, including the specific research content and data employed throughout the article, as well as the right to retain attribution rights as the article's original creator and writer.

Licensing Transfer

As the sole licensee of your article, SHERM retains the exclusive right to publish, distribute, or transfer the license of your article to other third parties for private and commercial purposes. SHERM reserves the right to create and authorize the commercial use of any and all published articles.

In order to make your published article available to as many audiences and researchers as possible, SHERM reserves the right to post (and repost even after initial publication of) your article in any form or media as allowable by the newest technological developments. Currently, this means SHERM will post your article to numerous open access websites and social media platforms. SHERM also reserves the right to advertise the publication of your article through various mediums.

By transferring exclusive licensing rights to SHERM, authors agree to the following stipulations:
- Authors cannot republish their article (either in English or in another language) with a different academic journal (without express consent from SHERM).
- Authors who repost their article online must incorporate a citation that indicates SHERM as the publisher of the content (including a link to the original article on the SHERM website, as well as the volume and issue number).
- Authors who wish to use portions of the article for other publications or work must cite the original SHERM publication.
- SHERM is granted authorization to impose copyright infringements laws, as well as combat instances of plagiarism against third parties on behalf of the author(s).

TABLE OF CONTENTS

VOLUME 1, No. 1
SPRING 2019

SHERM 1/1 (2019): 1–9

Grenz and Franke's Post-Foundationalism and the Religion Singularity

Jeshua B. Branch,
Liberty University Online Academy

Abstract: Termed the "religion singularity" by Kenneth Howard, the habitual fragmentation of institutional Christianity has led to the exponential growth in denominations and worship centers despite the annual growth rate of new believers remaining the same. Howard has concluded that denominations are unlikely to survive this crisis, although worship centers are much more likely to survive if they are willing to be flexible. The purpose of this article is to identify the epistemic trends that have led to the destabilization of institutional Christianity over the last century, namely the shifting worldview from modernity to postmodernity, and how this shift has influenced the rise of nondenominational house church attendance in American Christianity.

Keywords: Foundationalism, Institutional Christianity, Nondenominational Churches, Religion Singularity, Postmodernity

Introduction

IN *TRANSFORMING MISSION*, DAVID Bosch identified and defined six epochs of Christianity that have taken shape in the past 2,000 years, the last of which he calls "the emerging, ecumenical paradigm." Bosch explains that Christians in each era believed they were faithful to God's intent for mission, but the individual paradigms were profoundly different.[1] Concerning the present era, Bosch writes, "The Christian church in general and the Christian mission in particular are today confronted with issues they have never even dreamt of and which are crying out for responses that are both relevant to the times and in harmony with the essence of the Christian faith."[2] Nearly thirty years later, Kenneth Howard identified one of these new and unforeseen quandaries facing effective Christian mission in what he calls the "religion singularity." The idea is based on Ray Kurzweil's prediction that "the exponentially increasing processing power of artificial/machine intelligence would overtake the rate of increase of unaugmented human intelligence by the mid-twenty-first century … and would mark the end of humanity as we know

---

[1] Bosch defines "mission" as referring "primarily to the *missio Dei* (God's mission), that is, God's self-revelation as the One who loves the world." He uses the term "Christian mission" to describe the participation of Christians in the *missio Dei*, such as engaging in the "realities of injustice, oppression, poverty, discrimination, and violence." He adds, "Mission includes evangelism as one of its essential dimensions [and is defined as] the proclamation of salvation in Christ to those who do not believe in him, calling them to repentance and conversion, announcing forgiveness of sin, and inviting them to become living members of Christ's earthly community and to begin a life of service to others in the power of the Holy Spirit" (David J. Bosch, *Transforming Mission: Paradigm Shifts in Theology of Mission* [Maryknoll, NY: Orbis Books, 1991], 10–11).

[2] Ibid., 188.

Socio-Historical Examination of Religion and Ministry
Volume 1, Issue 1, Spring 2019 www.shermjournal.org
© *Wipf and Stock Publishers. All Rights Reserved.*
Permissions: shermeditor@gmail.com
ISSN 2637-7519 (print), ISSN 2637-7500 (online)
https://doi.org/10.33929/sherm.2019.vol1.no1.01 (article)

WIPF *and*
STOCK
Publishers

it."[3] In brief, Howard corresponds "singularity" to the exponential surge in Christian denominations and worship centers, especially in the last one hundred years. Noting that since the worldwide Christian growth rate is projected to remain the same, Howard forecasts a dramatic transformation of institutional Christianity.[4] Due to these projections and more, present-day Christians are forced to ask if their faith can survive in this latest epoch. Howard believes survival is possible, but only if the fragmentation of Christianity subsides. Thus, he recommends Christian leaders experiment with less building-centric worship centers.

The purpose of this article is to explain the epistemic undercurrents of the "religion singularity" as it pertains to the current era of Christian mission. In particular, twenty-first century Christians are observing the transition of its faith into a new epoch based on the shifting from modernity to postmodernity. After summarizing Howard's findings, the article will identify how this shifting worldview has also induced a change from the epistemic system of foundationalism to post-foundationalism, as well as how the change can produce the possibility for Christian mission to continue despite the collapse of institutional Christianity. In fact, recent trends in American Protestantism suggest that nondenominational house churches will become increasingly prominent in the post-foundationalist era.

A Summary of the Religion Singularity

Howard first explains that institutional Christianity is in a state of crisis. At the turn of the twentieth century, Christianity was represented by 1,600 denominations; but by the 1950s, there were 9,300.[5] Within just fifty years, Christianity split into six times the amount of denominations than it had in its first nineteen centuries of existence. The number continued to accelerate, becoming 34,200 at the turn of the twenty-first century and it grew even more to 45,000 by 2014.[6] It has been projected that either the influx of Christian denominations will plateau at 97,000 by the year 2100 or it will continue to accelerate to 240,000.[7] At the same time, the total number of worship centers has exponentially grown, as well. From approximately 400,000 centers in 1900 to one million in 1950, the number continued to climb to 3.5 million at the turn of the century and exceeded 4.7 million by 2014. It is also projected that the number of worship centers will grow to 7.5 million by 2025 and reach 66.3 million by the year 2100.[8]

What makes these numbers significant is that while the annual growth rate for Christianity continues to remain the same (1.32% growth), the number of believers is exceeded by both the growth in number of denominations (1.98%) and worship centers (2.4%).[9] Thus, the worldwide Christian population growth rate is 33% less than denominational fragmentation and 41% below the spread of worship centers. In the twentieth century alone, the number of denominational members dropped from 349,000 to 58,000 and may continue to decrease to 17,500 (95% less) by the end of the twenty-first century. Likewise, the number of Christian

---

[3] Kenneth W. Howard, "The Religion Singularity: A Demographic Crisis Destabilizing and Transforming Institutional Christianity," *International Journal of Religion and Spirituality in Society* 7, no. 2 (2017): 77, http://dx.doi.org/10.18848/2154-8633/cgp/v07i02/77-93.

[4] Ibid., 77–78.

[5] Ibid., 82.

[6] Ibid.

[7] Ibid., 83.

[8] Ibid., 83–84.

[9] Ibid., 84.

congregants per worship center has dropped from 1,395 to just 64 during the twentieth century.[10] These numbers are noteworthy when considering they comprise the total worldwide Christian population, including those not associated with a worship center or denomination. The numbers would actually be more destabilizing if they counted only denominational memberships.

Regardless, Howard proposes that the rapid fragmentation of Christianity will eventually lead to its institutional collapse. He employs the mathematical and technological term "singularity" to describe this phenomenon, which signifies "the point at which the results of an equation exceed finite limitation, accelerating toward infinity but never reaching it, such as when a constant is divided by numbers approaching zero."[11] Here, singularity involves three distinct states: a slow take off, rapid acceleration, and finally the point of no return ("singularity").[12] He predicts that denominations may not survive the singularity phenomenon, although worship centers may survive if they are willing to be more experimental and flexible in their operations.[13]

Understanding Religion Singularity

The data from Howard's article expresses the evolution of the Christian religion as it attempts to meet the unique needs of an increasingly postmodern world. Christianity has, in fact, gone through notable shifts in its history with the stated intention of being socially and spiritually effective. For many leaders, Christians should not be dismayed as new, unforeseen obstacles arise like the institutional crisis described by the religion singularity. As Christopher Wright reflects, "[Christians] may be challenged by swimming in the postmodern pool, but we need not feel out of our depth there."[14] The question then becomes, What exactly has Howard identified epistemically with the singularity effect? This section will attempt to address the question by identifying how a foundationalist epistemology had influenced institutional Christianity and how reactions to foundationalism eventually led to the religion singularity.

Foundationalist Influences on the Religion Singularity

In *Beyond Foundationalism: Shaping Theology in a Postmodern Context*, Stanley Grenz and John Franke surveyed the historical and theological factors that may have led to the fragmentation of denominational Christianity. The authors explain how the postmodern context of the twenty-first century has characteristically rejected the foundationalism that typified Enlightenment epistemology, resulting in a post-foundationalist religiosity.[15] Based on their understanding of the paradigm shift from modernity to postmodernity, as well as from foundationalism to post-foundationalism, future researchers can determine the epistemic undercurrent that may have resulted in the institutional destabilization of the Christian religion.

---

[10] Howard, "The Religion Singularity," 85.

[11] Ibid., 80.

[12] Ibid.

[13] Ibid., 87.

[14] Christopher J. H. Wright, *The Mission of God: Unlocking the Bible's Grand Narrative* (Downers Grove, IL: InterVarsity Press, 2006), 46.

[15] Stanley J. Grenz and John R. Franke, *Beyond Foundationalism: Shaping Theology in a Postmodern Context* (Louisville, KY: Westminster John Knox Press, 2001), 28.

To begin, the Enlightenment became known as the "Age of Reason" and was significantly influenced by the philosophical work of René Descartes, who sought a "foundation" from which to construct all knowledge. He doubted everything he believed to be true until he determined that the only thing he could be certain of was his own existence, resulting in his famous dictum, "I think, therefore, I am."[16] A major consequence of Descartes' doubting was the epistemic system of foundationalism. This bottom-up approach to knowledge holds that some beliefs are more basic ("foundational") than others, making the entire system consist of three primary features: 1) basic beliefs form the bedrock of all future nonbasic beliefs; 2) these nonbasic beliefs derive from the indisputability of the basic beliefs; and 3) the subsequent nonbasic beliefs then receive the same epistemic certainty as their foundational counterparts. Here, the foundationalist goal is to ground the entire edifice of human knowledge upon invincible and incorrigible certainty.[17]

Soon, Christians adopted epistemic foundationalism and manifested its effects in different ways during the nineteenth and twentieth centuries. On the one hand, the foundation of theological liberalism emphasized the experience of individual believers, while on the other, the foundation of theological conservatism emphasized an inerrant Bible that held infallible historical and spiritual truths. As each side averred that their particular foundation was epistemically superior to the other, a schism occurred in Western Protestant Christianity.[18] Eventually, the evangelical movement's adoption of foundationalism built its own edifice upon a narrow sense of orthodoxy, which produced "fundamentalist" Christians who adhered to a legalistic system defined by its dissociation from the culture (e.g. abstaining from alcohol and movie theaters). While they professed theological orthodoxy, these (neo-)evangelicals distanced themselves from humanitarian efforts (i.e. the Social Gospel) because of a fear of compromising orthodoxy with liberalism and the perceived threat of de-emphasizing personal piety.[19]

Ultimately, Grenz and Franke concluded that this style of theological foundationalism had intensified theological divides, eventually leading to a cascade of Christian fragmentation. "Today we find significant differences not only between these two groups but also within them, differences regarding a host of theological issues."[20] The natural result of this fragmentation is the exponential increase in denominations and worship centers (the "religion singularity"). Thus, the effect of Christianity rapidly fragmenting into competing institutions has become more noticeable as the current epistemic paradigm shift into post-foundationalism has forced some believers to reimagine the nature of "effective" Christian mission in the twenty-first century.

---

[16] Grenz and Franke, *Beyond Foundationalism*, 31.

[17] Ibid., 30. See also, Ferdinand Deist, "Post-Modernism and the Use of Scripture in Theological Argument: Footnotes to the Apartheid Theology Debate," *Neotestamentica* 28, no. 3 (1994): 253–63.

[18] Grenz and Franke, *Beyond Foundationalism*, 33–38.

[19] Significantly, by the last quarter of the twentieth century, evangelical scholars and theologians began to take very seriously the importance of social justice by balancing their former overt emphasis on conversion. This trend has positively affected the missional practice of (post-)conservatives in the twenty-first century. Cf. Frank E. Gaebelein, "Evangelicals and Social Concern," *Journal of the Evangelical Theological Society* 25, no. 1 (March 1982): 17–22; Brian Steensland and Philip Goff, eds., *The New Evangelical Social Engagement* (New York: Oxford University Press, 2014), 1, https://doi.org/10.1093/acprof:oso/9780199329533.001.0001; Ronald J. Sider, "Evangelicals and Social Justice," in *Evangelicals Around the World: A Global Handbook for the 21st Century*, ed. Brian C. Stiller et al. (Nashville, TN: Thomas Nelson, 2015), 128–33; and David P. Gushee and Justin Phillips, "Moral Formation and the Evangelical Voter: A Report from the Red States," *Journal of the Society of Christian Ethics* 26, no. 2 (2006): 23–60, https://doi.org/10.5840/jsce20062623.

[20] Grenz and Franke, *Beyond Foundationalism*, 4.

An Epistemic Transition

Over the course of the last century, and especially in the last several decades, foundationalism has increasingly lost its influence on Western culture. A growing number of scholars have recognized the growth and popularity of postmodernity and its post-foundationalist approach to religion.[21] Significantly, post-foundationalism does not rebuff the fundamental idea of foundationalism that certain (basic) beliefs can act as an anchor for other derived beliefs. For example, some evangelical philosophers, such as Alvin Plantinga, reject the idea of "strong foundationalism" because it relegates religious belief to a nonbasic status. However, these philosophers "do not deny categorically the validity of the foundationalist search for basic beliefs."[22] Rather, they view the church as its own properly basic epistemic community from which to construct Christian theology.[23]

In contrast to the effects of the Enlightenment, where theology became a strictly academic affair, post-foundationalists now seek to return theology back to the church, believing that Christian theology is "an activity of the community that gathers around Jesus the Christ."[24] Accordingly, post-foundational theology may be understood as a mosaic or tapestry that more graciously embraces softly opposing theological differences (e.g. spiritual gifts, mode of baptism, etc.) rather than allow peripheral issues to cause division.[25] Post-foundational churches will therefore be more specifically characterized by the collective theological background of its members rather than a commitment to one particular denomination. Hence, the decreasing amount of denominational commitment and the exponential increase of worship centers are likely to result, in part, from a gradually post-foundational theological epistemology.[26]

Responding to the Religion Singularity

Trends in American Protestantism already demonstrate significant changes in the commitment of individuals to particular denominational affiliations based on the following

---

[21] Grenz and Franke, *Beyond Foundationalism*, 38–42, 46. Cf. K. F. Godfrey, "Postfoundationalist Rationality and Progress in the Theology of Religious Conversion," *The Asia Journal of Theology* 20, no. 1 (April 2006): 142–54 and Deist, "Post-Modernism and the Use of Scripture," 253–63.

[22] Grenz and Franke, *Beyond Foundationalism*, 47. See for example, Alvin Plantinga, "Reason and Belief in God," in *Faith and Rationality: Reason and Belief in God*, ed. Alvin Plantinga and Nicholas Wolterstorff (Notre Dame, IN: University of Notre Dame Press, 1983), 16–93.

[23] Cf. Archie J. Spencer, "Culture, Community and Commitments: Stanley J. Grenz on Theological Method," *Scottish Journal of Theology* 57, no. 3 (2004): 338–60, http://dx.doi.org/10.1017/s0036930604000274.

[24] Grenz and Franke, *Beyond Foundationalism*, 48.

[25] Darren M. Slade, "Religious Homophily and Biblicism: A Theory of Conservative Church Fragmentation," *The International Journal of Religion and Spirituality in Society* 9, no. 1 (2019): 13–28, http://dx.doi.org/10.18848/2154-8633/cgp/v09i01/13-28. While foundational theology could be portrayed as the steps required to build a house (for example, by first laying a foundation and building upon it), post-foundational theology is understood as a systemic body working in unison to accomplish effective ministry. See John R. Franke, *The Character of Theology: An Introduction to Its Nature, Task, and Purpose* (Grand Rapids, MI: Baker Academic, 2005), 30.

[26] Cf. Jan-Olav Henriksen, "Researching Theological Normativity: Some Critical and Constructive Suggestions," *Studia Theologica* 60, no. 2 (2006): 207–20, http://dx.doi.org/10.1080/00393380601010185 and M. C. de Lange, "Reflections on Methodology and Interdisciplinarity in the Postmodern Dialogue between Theology and the Natural Sciences," *Acta Theologica* 27, no. 2 (2007): 44–62, http://dx.doi.org/10.4314/actat.v27i2.5499.

factors: 1) the long-term decline of membership in liberal-leaning denominations; 2) the short-term plateau or decline of membership in conservative denominations despite long-term increases; and 3) the short-term growth of nondenominational membership.[27] Since the 1970s, Protestant Christianity has decreased in percentage of the U.S. population from 62% to 51%, though it has grown numerically by 28 million people.[28] The change is linked, in part, to the long-term decline of mainline denominations while congregations with a more conservative theology have seen steady increases.[29] For instance, the United Church of Christ (Congregationalist), a traditionally mainline denomination, has seen a decline of 52% from 2,070,413 members in 1965 to 998,906 members in 2012. Likewise, the Presbyterian Church (U.S.A.) decreased by 47% from 3,304,321 members to 1,760,200 during the same time span. On the other hand, conservative groups like The Church of God in Christ has increased by 1,194% in membership. Other more conservative denominations include the Presbyterian Church in America with a 790% increase and the Southern Baptist Convention at 46%.[30]

Nevertheless, more recent research demonstrates a decreasing commitment of American Christians to both mainline and non-mainline congregations. The Office of the General Assembly for the Presbyterian Church (U.S.A.) shows that the declining number of members has slowed (but not stopped entirely). The most recent statistics in 2017 show a net loss of nearly 68,000 members since 2016, leaving the new total at 1,415,053.[31] Also, the status of the United Church of Christ membership is currently 853,778 (-1.2%) since 2012.[32] Equally, conservative evangelical groups have seen plateaued or declining membership from 2007 to 2014. During these years, Pentecostal and Adventist groups have grown minimally at +0.2% and +0.1% respectively, whereas others have seen slight decreases, such as Restorationists (-0.2%) and Holiness (-0.4%) groups. Baptist denominations had the greatest loss among conservatives with a decrease of 1.8%, though mainline groups collectively decreased by 3.6% total.[33]

Today, post-liberal and post-conservative Christians have each taken strides to overcome the detrimental effects of foundationalism and to revise Christian mission in a postmodern context. The former has been influential in the cultivation of Emergence Christianity (EC) and the latter for what is a type of missional church planting movement. Both practice postmodern ministry by embracing a post-foundational religiosity, which attempts to halt theological division at the congregational level. In fact, the mounting influence of EC and missional church planting may correlate to the increase in nondenominational church

---

[27] See Roger Finke and Rodney Stark, *The Churching of America, 1776–2005: Winners and Losers in Our Religious Economy* (New Brunswick, NJ: Rutgers University Press, 2005), 156–283.

[28] Joe Carter, "Factchecker: Are All Christian Denominations in Decline?," The Gospel Coalition, March 17, 2015, thegospelcoalition.org/article/factchecker-are-all-christian-denominations-in-decline/.

[29] Cf. David Millard Haskell, Kevin N. Flatt, and Stephanie Burgoyne, "Theology Matters: Comparing the Traits of Growing and Declining Mainline Protestant Church Attendees and Clergy," *Review of Religious Research* 58, no. 4 (2016): 515–41, http://dx.doi.org/10.1007/s13644-016-0255-4 and Laurence R. Iannaccone, "Why Strict Churches Are Strong," *American Journal of Sociology* 99, no. 5 (1994): 1180–1211, http://dx.doi.org/10.1086/230409.

[30] Carter, "Factchecker."

[31] See Presbyterian Church (USA), *2017 Comparative Summaries* (Louisville, KY: Office of the General Assembly 2017), oga.pcusa.org/section/churchwide-ministries/stats/denominational-statistics/.

[32] See *United Church of Christ: A Statistical Profile* (Cleveland, OH: UCC, 2018), https://www.uccfiles.com/pdf/2018-UCC-Statistical-Profile.pdf.

[33] Gregory Smith, *America's Changing Religious Landscape: Christians Decline Sharply as Share of Population; Unaffiliated and Other Faiths Continue to Grow* (Washington, DC: Pew Research Center, May 12, 2015), accessed March 26, 2019, https://www.pewforum.org/2015/05/12/americas-changing-religious-landscape/.

attendance.[34] In the U.S., for example, 194,000 people attended a nondenominational church in 1990, but this demographic significantly increased to 8 million by 2008.[35] Research also shows that nondenominational church affiliation continued to increase from 2007 to 2014 by 1.7% among all U.S. adults and 4% among Protestants.[36] This increase appears to parallel the increase in Christians who are at least sympathetic to the postmodern matrix.[37]

With the steady growth of the religiously unaffiliated, however, adherents of post-foundational nondenominational churches will likely need to emphasize both the need for missional practices (e.g. addressing social injustice, poverty, and violence), as well as effective proselytizing tactics to restabilize the Christian church.[38] During this process, it is important to note Howard's belief that church leaders should experiment with less building-centric worship centers in order to overcome the collapse of institutional Christianity.[39] With this in mind, it is suggestive that house churches are increasingly becoming a viable option for such experimentation. In fact, house churches are growing with over one-quarter (26.3%) of American Christians in 2009 meeting in private homes instead of traditional church buildings.[40] For many, in fact, the house church movement offers a needed corrective to American religiosity that allows for a more simplistic and community-oriented approach to Christian faith.[41]

Conclusion

As institutional Christianity enters more fully into its latest ecumenical epoch, there will be significant alterations that rightly cause many to ask if the Christian religion can still thrive or even survive. Kenneth Howard notes that the collapse of institutional Christianity will be one of the most crucial obstacles for believers to overcome. Although the religion will likely appear very different in the near future from its institutionalized past, Christians still have the potential to maximize their effectiveness in the postmodern context. In particular, post-foundational

---

[34] For details on the EC movement, see Michael Clawson and April Stace, eds., *Crossing Boundaries, Redefining Faith: Interdisciplinary Perspectives On the Emerging Church Movement* (Eugene, OR: Pickwick Publications, 2016). Cf. Mark S. Medley, "Catholics, Baptists, and the Normativity of Tradition: A Review Essay," *Perspectives in Religious Studies* 28, no. 2 (Summer 2001): 119–29.

[35] Scott Thumma, *A Report On the 2010 National Profile of U.S. Nondenominational and Independent Churches* (Hartford, CT: Hartford Institute for Religion Research, 2010), http://hirr.hartsem.edu/cong/nondenominational-churches-national-profile-2010.html.

[36] See Smith, *America's Changing Religious Landscape.*

[37] Cf. Stanley Hauerwas, Nancey C. Murphy, and Mark Nation, eds., *Theology Without Foundations: Religious Practice and the Future of Theological Truth* (Nashville, TN: Abingdon Press, 1994) and Nancey C. Murphy, *Beyond Liberalism and Fundamentalism: How Modern and Postmodern Philosophy Set the Theological Agenda*(Valley Forge, PA: Trinity Press International, 1996).

[38] Bosch identifies both as quintessential in what has defined proper mission in every paradigm (Bosch, *Transforming Mission*, 8–11).

[39] Howard, "The Religion Singularity," 87.

[40] Ed Stetzer, "Counting People Who Attend House Churches," *Christianity Today*, September 3, 2009, https://www.christianitytoday.com/edstetzer/2009/september/counting-people-who-attend-house-churches.html.

[41] Cf. Jervis David Payne, "A Glimpse into the Missional House Churches of America," *Journal of the American Society for Church Growth* 19 (Winter 2008): 87–98 and Rad Zdero, "The Apostolic Strategy of House Churches for Mission Today," *Evangelical Missions Quarterly* 47, no. 3 (July 2011): 346–53.

churches will need to take account of the epistemic shifts occurring in theology and identify how to maintain a stable identity while denominations and congregations continue to fragment around them. Of course, only time will tell whether the epistemic change from foundationalism to post-foundationalism will, in fact, curb the rapid division occurring in Christianity or if it will only proliferate the ever-increasing percentage of religious "nones" in the world.

BIBLIOGRAPHY

Bosch, David J. *Transforming Mission: Paradigm Shifts in Theology of Mission*. Maryknoll, NY: Orbis Books, 1991.

Carter, Joe. "Factchecker: Are All Christian Denominations in Decline?" The Gospel Coalition. March 17, 2015. www.thegospelcoalition.org/article/factchecker-are-all-christian-denominations-in-decline/.

Clawson, Michael, and April Stace, eds. *Crossing Boundaries, Redefining Faith: Interdisciplinary Perspectives On the Emerging Church Movement*. Eugene, OR: Pickwick Publications, 2016.

de Lange, M. C. "Reflections on Methodology and Interdisciplinarity in the Postmodern Dialogue between Theology and the Natural Sciences." *Acta Theologica* 27, no. 2 (2007): 44–62. http://dx.doi.org/10.4314/actat.v27i2.5499.

Deist, Ferdinand. "Post-Modernism and the Use of Scripture in Theological Argument: Footnotes to the Apartheid Theology Debate." *Neotestamentica* 28, no. 3 (1994): 253–63.

Finke, Roger, and Rodney Stark. *The Churching of America, 1776–2005: Winners and Losers in Our Religious Economy*. New Brunswick, NJ: Rutgers University Press, 2005.

Franke, John R. *The Character of Theology: An Introduction to Its Nature, Task, and Purpose*. Grand Rapids, MI: Baker Academic, 2005.

Gaebelein, Frank E. "Evangelicals and Social Concern." *Journal of the Evangelical Theological Society* 25, no. 1 (March 1982): 17–22.

Godfrey, K. F. "Postfoundationalist Rationality and Progress in the Theology of Religious Conversion." *The Asia Journal of Theology* 20, no. 1 (April 2006): 142–54.

Grenz, Stanley J., and John R. Franke. *Beyond Foundationalism: Shaping Theology in a Postmodern Context*. Louisville, KY: Westminster John Knox Press, 2001.

Gushee, David P., and Justin Phillips. "Moral Formation and the Evangelical Voter: A Report from the Red States." *Journal of the Society of Christian Ethics* 26, no. 2 (2006): 23–60. https://doi.org/10.5840/jsce20062623.

Haskell, David Millard, Kevin N. Flatt, and Stephanie Burgoyne. "Theology Matters: Comparing the Traits of Growing and Declining Mainline Protestant Church Attendees and Clergy." *Review of Religious Research* 58, no. 4 (2016): 515–41. http://dx.doi.org/10.1007/s13644-016-0255-4.

Hauerwas, Stanley, Nancey C. Murphy, and Mark Nation, eds. *Theology Without Foundations: Religious Practice and the Future of Theological Truth*. Nashville, TN: Abingdon Press, 1994.

Henriksen, Jan-Olav. "Researching Theological Normativity: Some Critical and Constructive Suggestions." *Studia Theologica* 60, no. 2 (2006): 207–20. http://dx.doi.org/10.1080/00393380601010185.

Howard, Kenneth W. "The Religion Singularity: A Demographic Crisis Destabilizing and Transforming Institutional Christianity." *International Journal of Religion and Spirituality in Society* 7, no. 2 (2017): 77–93. http://dx.doi.org/10.18848/2154-8633/cgp/v07i02/77-93.

Iannaccone, Laurence R. "Why Strict Churches Are Strong." *American Journal of Sociology* 99, no. 5 (1994): 1180–1211. http://dx.doi.org/10.1086/230409.

Medley, Mark S. "Catholics, Baptists, and the Normativity of Tradition: A Review Essay." *Perspectives in Religious Studies* 28, no. 2 (Summer 2001): 119–29.

Murphy, Nancey C. *Beyond Liberalism and Fundamentalism: How Modern and Postmodern Philosophy Set the Theological Agenda*. Valley Forge, PA: Trinity Press International, 1996.

Payne, Jervis David. "A Glimpse into the Missional House Churches of America." *Journal of the American Society for Church Growth* 19 (Winter 2008): 87–98.

Plantinga, Alvin. "Reason and Belief in God." In *Faith and Rationality: Reason and Belief in God*, edited by Alvin Plantinga and Nicholas Wolterstorff, 16–93. Notre Dame, IN: University of Notre Dame Press, 1983.

Presbyterian Church (USA). *2017 Comparative Summaries*. Louisville, KY: Office of the General Assembly, 2017. oga.pcusa.org/section/churchwide-ministries/stats/denominational-statistics/.

Sider, Ronald J. "Evangelicals and Social Justice." In *Evangelicals Around the World: A Global Handbook for the 21st Century*, edited by Brian C. Stiller et al, 128–33. Nashville, TN: Thomas Nelson, 2015.

Slade, Darren M. "Religious Homophily and Biblicism: A Theory of Conservative Church Fragmentation." *The International Journal of Religion and Spirituality in Society* 9, no. 1 (2019): 13–28. http://dx.doi.org/10.18848/2154-8633/cgp/v09i01/13-28.

Smith, Gregory. *America's Changing Religious Landscape: Christians Decline Sharply as Share of Population; Unaffiliated and Other Faiths Continue to Grow*. Washington, DC: Pew Research Center, May 12, 2015. Accessed March 26, 2019. https://www.pewforum.org/2015/05/12/americas-changing-religious-landscape/.

Spencer, Archie J. "Culture, Community and Commitments: Stanley J. Grenz on Theological Method." *Scottish Journal of Theology* 57, no. 3 (2004): 338–60. http://dx.doi.org/10.1017/s0036930604000274.

Steensland, Brian, and Philip Goff, eds. *The New Evangelical Social Engagement*. New York: Oxford University Press, 2014. doi.org/10.1093/acprof:oso/9780199329533.001.0001.

Stetzer, Ed. "Counting People Who Attend House Churches." *Christianity Today*, September 3, 2009. https://www.christianitytoday.com/edstetzer/2009/september/counting-people-who-attend-house-churches.html.

Thumma, Scott. *A Report On the 2010 National Profile of U.S. Nondenominational and Independent Churches*. Hartford, CT: Hartford Institute for Religion Research, 2010. hirr.hartsem.edu/cong/nondenominational-churches-national-profile-2010.html.

United Church of Christ: A Statistical Profile. Cleveland, OH: UCC, 2018. https://www.uccfiles.com/pdf/2018-UCC-Statistical-Profile.pdf.

Wright, Christopher J. H. *The Mission of God: Unlocking the Bible's Grand Narrative*. Downers Grove, IL: InterVarsity Press, 2006.

Zdero, Rad. "The Apostolic Strategy of House Churches for Mission Today." *Evangelical Missions Quarterly* 47, no. 3 (July 2011): 346–53.

ABOUT THE AUTHOR

Jeshua B. Branch earned his Ph.D. in theology and apologetics from Liberty University. He is passionate about inspiring Christians to live faithfully on mission for Jesus Christ in a postmodern world. He lives in Williamsburg, VA and is married to his college sweetheart, Megan. Together, they have 3 daughters: Elena, Elora, and Eliza.

ACKNOWLEDGEMENT

I would like to thank Darren Slade and the Editorial Advisory Board of SHERM journal for the opportunity to contribute to its first issue.

First Century Christian Diversity:
Historical Evidence of a Social Phenomenon

John F. Lingelbach,
Rawlings School of Divinity (Liberty University)

Abstract: In light of Ken Howard's recent "religion singularity" phenomenon, this article attempts to ascertain the nature of Christian diversity during the last seventy years of the first century (roughly 30 to 100 CE). It offers an examination of the two largest Christian movements that existed before the second century, as well as when those movements may have begun and the locations they most likely flourished. The article argues that the earliest Christian tradition was the one persecuted by the Apostle Paul and that later, two breakaway movements splintered off from this tradition: the Pauline and Ebionite movements. The paper concludes that during the first century, of these two splinter movements, the Pauline movement likely preceded that of the Ebionite movement, though they both flourished in many of the same locations. Of interest is the finding that all three Christian movements (the pre-Pauline tradition, Pauline, and Ebionite) flourished in Asia Minor, a cosmopolitan sub-continent which appears to have served as a geographic information nucleus through which diverse ideas easily proliferated.

Keywords: Christianity, Church Demographics, Christian Diversity, First Century Church,
 Religion Singularity

Introduction

ACCORDING TO KENNETH HOWARD, present-day institutional Christianity is experiencing a sociological phenomenon which he terms the "religion singularity."[1] The phenomenon consists of a global expansion in the number of "new and breakaway" denominations or movements.[2] This explosion of movements outpaces the overall growth rate of the Christian population in a way that, according to Howard, has apparently never happened before in the history of the religion and may result in a change significant enough to be considered a paradigm shift.[3] In addition, Howard concludes that because these various new movements will presumably be different in nature from one another, a new age of Christian diversity may be on the horizon, harkening back to the diversity of the first century, a time during which Howard contends there were "many Christianities."[4]

---

[1] Kenneth W. Howard, "The Religion Singularity: A Demographic Crisis Destabilizing and Transforming Institutional Christianity," *International Journal of Religion and Spirituality in Society* 7, no. 2 (2017): 77–93, http://dx.doi.org/10.18848/2154-8633/cgp/v07i02/77-93.

[2] Ibid., 90.

[3] Ibid., 77, 78, 88, 90.

[4] Howard, "The Religion Singularity," 87, 90. Elsewhere, Howard notes two genera of Christianity in the first century, which he designates "The Nazarene Jewish Christian Movement" and "The Pauline Gentile Christianity Movement" (Ken Howard, *Paradoxy: Creating Christian Community Beyond Us and Them* [Brewster, MA: Paraclete Press, 2010], 67–76).

Socio-Historical Examination of Religion and Ministry
Volume 1, Issue 1, Spring 2019 www.shermjournal.org
© *Wipf and Stock Publishers. All Rights Reserved.*
Permissions: shermeditor@gmail.com
ISSN 2637-7519 (print), ISSN 2637-7500 (online)
https://doi.org/10.33929/sherm.2019.vol1.no1.02 (article)

WIPF *and*
STOCK
Publishers

Howard is not the only scholar who has studied the varieties of Christianity in the early church. In his landmark work, *Orthodoxy and Heresy in Earliest Christianity*, theologian and scholar, Walter Bauer, described a number of Christian movements that prevailed in the second century.[5] Interestingly, Bauer chose not to consider New Testament literature as a source for his investigation, and he altogether omitted inquiry into the mid-first century.[6] Similarly New Testament scholar and church historian, Bart Ehrman, catalogued "the wide diversity of early Christianity."[7] Here, Ehrman focused on second and third century variations in Christian theology.[8] Furthermore, Everett Ferguson, in his edited volume *Doctrinal Diversity: Varieties of Early Christianity*, concedes that this diversity was "present from [Christianity's] beginning and continuing even after orthodoxy was firmly institutionalized."[9] Ferguson's volume consists of essays from a number of scholars which deal with diverse Christian teachings from the second century and later.

Much like the aforementioned studies, this article also examines diversity in early Christianity; but, in consideration of Howard's comparison between the twenty-first and first century church, it takes on the task of investigating how Christian diversity manifested itself during that *earliest* period (i.e. from about 30 to 100 CE). This research is important because understanding the similarities and differences between the "Christianities" of the very earliest era furnishes students of religion with an historical foundation upon which to construct subsequent understandings of the social and theological history of the church. Conducting such research should lead to a more accurate knowledge of which Christian elements (if any) were primary, which of these teachings persevered, and which were abandoned. This may also prompt further investigation into *why* certain elements were retained or jettisoned.[10] In short, the research should lend to a greater comprehension of how Christianity evolved from its earliest traditions and the degree to which scholars can reasonably consider those elements paradigmatic to pre-Pauline Christianity. Moreover, this research is necessary because it will help temper assertions that may exaggerate the degree to which first century Christianity was either diverse or unified in its beliefs. An investigation of this type is relevant due to the current cultural emphasis on religious pluralism and diversity.

This article, therefore, offers an examination of the two main movements that broke away from the earliest detectable traditions of the Jesus movement, as well as when those movements may have begun and the locations they most likely flourished. It argues that the

---

[5] Walter Bauer, *Rechtgläubigkeit Und Ketzerei Im Ältesten Christentum* [Orthodoxy and Heresy in Earliest Christianity], 2nd ed., ed. Georg Strecker, Beiträge zur Historischen Theologie 10 (Tübingen, Germany: Mohr [Siebeck], 1963), 5.

[6] Ibid., 3, 5, 81–98. Bauer dealt with those doctrines that emerged in Asia Minor toward the end of the first century, such as those mentioned in John's Apocalypse and those in the Pastorals, but these doctrines likely did not precede the pre-Pauline or Pauline traditions which manifested in the late 30s and 40s CE. Bauer also treats the topics of Marcionism, Gnosticism, and other diverse doctrines in Edessa, but it is more likely that these emerged and flourish in the second century rather than in the first.

[7] Bart D. Ehrman, *Lost Christianities: The Battle for Scripture and the Faiths We Never Knew* (New York: Oxford University Press, 2003), ix.

[8] Ibid., 2–3. Specifically, Ehrman focused on Ebionism, Marcionism, Gnosticism, and Montanism. The last three of these are deemed by scholars to have flourished in the second century. Ebionism is treated in this present paper as one of the first century Christianities, though it is likely not the earliest.

[9] Everett Ferguson, ed., "Volume Introduction," in *Doctrinal Diversity: Varieties of Early Christianity*, Recent Studies in Early Christianity 4 (New York: Garland Publishing, 1999), ix.

[10] See also, Arland J. Hultgren, *The Rise of Normative Christianity* (Minneapolis, MN: Fortress Press, 1994), 7-18.

earliest Christian tradition was the one persecuted by the Apostle Paul and that later, two breakaway movements splintered off from this tradition: the Pauline and Ebionite movements. The paper concludes that during the first century, of these two splinter movements, the Pauline movement likely preceded the Ebionite movement, though they both flourished in many of the same locations. Of interest is the finding that all three Christian movements (the pre-Pauline tradition, Pauline, and Ebionite) flourished in Asia Minor, a cosmopolitan sub-continent which appears to have served as a geographic nucleus through which diverse ideas easily proliferated.

The Pre-Pauline Oral Tradition

In his Epistle to the Galatians, the Apostle Paul offers evidence for a pre-Pauline oral tradition when he mentions "the faith he once tried to destroy" (Gal. 1:23, NRSV).[11] This "faith" would have had to exist prior to Paul's conversion, which likely took place two to three years after Jesus's crucifixion (ca. 30).[12] Paul probably received an introduction to this initial version of Christianity from Peter and James three years after his conversion (that is, ca. 35 to 36).[13] Ehrman is emphatic about this and highlights the timing by stating, "I should stress . . . that Paul indicates on several occasions that the traditions about Jesus are ones that he himself inherited from those who came *before* him."[14] There are no extant recordings of any other form of Christianity during the period between the crucifixion and Paul's conversion, though some core elements of the oral tradition may be discernable in Paul's writings, particularly through primitive creeds.[15]

In addition, Paul suggests he had appropriated this oral tradition for himself. According to his Galatian Epistle, Christians in Judaea had heard, "The one [i.e. Paul] who formerly was persecuting us is now proclaiming the faith" (Gal. 1:23). The text suggests that Paul had subscribed to and began proclaiming this earlier oral tradition from the years 36 to 40 because, as Ehrman suggests, Aretas (d. ca. 40), the king of the Nabateans, sought to kill Paul because of his newfound faith (2 Cor. 11:31–2).[16] However, Eric Eve cautions that the evidence must not be pressed too much since "this is, of course, more directly a statement about what Paul wanted his Galatian audience to believe than what actually happened."[17] Based on this, it is possible that Paul adopted the earliest oral traditions about Jesus, at least initially.

---

[11] Howard, *Paradoxy*, 72. This article draws data from the least disputed texts of the Pauline Epistles (the *Hauptebriefe*), namely 1 Thessalonians, Galatians, 1 and 2 Corinthians, and Romans.

[12] Bart D. Ehrman, *Did Jesus Exist? The Historical Argument for Jesus of Nazareth*, Pbk. ed. (2012; repr., New York: HarperOne, 2013), 130–31. Ehrman places Paul's conversion around 32 or 33 CE, and Jesus's crucifixion around 30 or 31.

[13] Ibid., 131, 143–45. See also, Eric Eve, *Behind the Gospels: Understanding the Oral Tradition* (2013; repr., Minneapolis, MN: Fortress Press, 2014), 159–69.

[14] Ibid., 129; emphasis added. See also, Gal. 1:17.

[15] Cf. J. N. D. Kelly, *Early Christian Creeds*, 3rd ed. (1950; repr., New York: Continuum International Publishing Group, 2011), 1–29, https://doi.org/10.4324/9781315836720 and Eve, *Behind the Gospels*, 159–69. While portions of the canonical gospels and the Acts of the Apostles cover the period between the crucifixion and Paul's conversion, their historicity is disputed by some scholars. Regardless, whether one accepts their accuracy or not, they do not attest to a form of Christianity that stands in *contradiction* to the version Paul would have persecuted.

[16] Ehrman, *Did Jesus Exist?*, 130.

[17] Eve, *Behind the Gospels*, 168.

It is also apparent that from about 35 to 49, pre-Pauline Christianity, to which Paul claimed to continue, saw the beginnings of a sophisticated Christology, to the extent that Martin Hengel suggests, "In essentials more happened in christology [sic] within these few years than in the whole subsequent seven hundred years of church history."[18] An example may be seen in Paul's identification of Jesus as "Christ," "Lord," and God's "Son" (Gal. 1:1, 3; 4:4). Paul also understood Jesus to have been raised "from the dead" (Gal. 1:1), who will return again one day (1 Thess. 1:10). According to Paul, he had not developed these christological assertions on his own, but rather had received them from others (1 Cor. 15:3), possibly from Peter and James, particularly the notion that Jesus had been raised from the dead.[19] Ehrman suggests that these traditions had been handed to Paul in much the same way rabbinic teaching was passed on and that they may have been the core of Paul's message.[20] That these christological features remained hallmarks of Paul's message until at least as late as the year 62 is borne out by similar declarations in his later Epistle to the Romans (written ca. 61–62). Here, Paul writes that Jesus "was declared to be Son of God with power according to the spirit of holiness by resurrection from the dead, Jesus Christ our Lord" (Rom. 1:4). Here, Paul cites an ancient creed that suggests continuity between his christological message and the earliest oral traditions.[21]

There is also reason to believe that this primitive Christian movement can be identified with, or at least closely associated with, a group of Christians known as the Nazarenes. The earliest implicit reference to the group appears in Justin Martyr's *Dialogue with Trypho*. Here, Justin describes fellowship with these Jewish Christians and contrasts them with those who do not believe in Christ's virgin birth (*Dial.* 47–48), potentially linking them to a more nuanced Christology that is later described in the Gospels of Matthew and Luke (ca. 80–85). The earliest explicit reference to the Nazarenes comes from Epiphanius (*Anc.* 13.3; *Pan.* 29), who stated they existed prior to the name "Christian" being assigned to disciples in Antioch, which means the Nazarenes may predate Paul's conversion (*Pan.* 29.1). That they predate the Ebionites is also apparent to Ray Pritz, who concludes, "We have little reason to doubt the other statements of Epiphanius which consistently tell us that the Ebionites were later than the Nazarenes."[22] Furthermore, if the testimony of the Acts of the Apostles (2:10) is to be believed, it may be that inductees to the movement were residents of Rome. If these inductees, having embraced a new messianic movement, returned to Rome and started a church in that city, then there exists a possible connection between Rome and the pre-Pauline oral traditions in Jerusalem.

From a demographic standpoint, how many of the earliest followers of Jesus existed or where their churches were located remains uncertain. Nevertheless, it is reasonable to believe, based on Paul's testimony in Galatians, that they began in Jerusalem (Gal. 1:18–2:10) and spread to Asia Minor, particularly the Galatian churches (1:1–3:1).[23] According to Rodney Stark, roughly five weeks after the crucifixion of Jesus to the year 40, the number of Christians in the

---

[18] Martin Hengel, *Between Jesus and Paul: Studies in the Earliest History of Christianity*, trans. John Bowden (Philadelphia, PA: Fortress Press, 1983), 39–40.

[19] Ehrman, *Did Jesus Exist?*, 118, 120–27; Eve, *Behind the Gospels*, 159–69. Concerning this pre-Pauline oral tradition, Howard asserts, "We know that it was diverse, including Jews from a wide variety of religious origins (from Pharisees to Sadducees to Essenes to proselytes), socioeconomic levels (from fishermen to members of the Sanhedrin), and national origins (from Judea to Egypt, and from Mesopotamia to Rome)" (Howard, *Paradoxy*, 70).

[20] Ehrman, *Did Jesus Exist?*, 118–25.

[21] Ibid., 118–19, 130.

[22] Ray A. Pritz, *Nazarene Jewish Christianity: From the End of the New Testament Period Until Its Disappearance in the Fourth Century* (Leiden, Netherlands: Brill, 1988), 38.

[23] Ehrman, *Did Jesus Exist?*, 130–31.

world grew from an initial 120 to 1,000.[24] A significant portion of this movement would have adhered to a pre-Pauline form of Christianity, likely having spread among congregations in Judaea, Syria, and Asia Minor (Gal. 1:2, 17, 21, 22; 2:11). It is possible that they spread further, but historians are uncertain how far the initial Jesus traditions proliferated.[25] Some patristic writers claimed adherents of these initial traditions also took up residence in Pella of the Decapolis across the Jordan River (Eusebius, *Hist. eccl.* 3.5.3; Epiphanius, *Pan.* 29.7; 30.2).[26]

In summary, the first of the oral traditions about Jesus existed as early as 30 CE and likely consisted of a Christology that regarded Jesus as the risen Christ, Lord, and Son of God. According to Paul's First Epistle to the Corinthians, the earliest leaders, such as Peter and James, passed this tradition on a few years after his conversion, though the precise content of what was passed on is unknown.[27] Adherents to this initial faith likely wielded influence in Judaea, Syria, and Asia Minor prior to 40. Paul claimed to embrace this tradition about Jesus for at least twenty-five years (i.e. from 35 to 61). However, during those years, Paul apparently developed his own modified form of Christianity, becoming the first noticeable breakaway from the earliest traditions. This "Pauline Christianity," while claiming to retain pre-Pauline beliefs, ended up abandoning certain Judaistic practices in order to proselytize Gentiles outside of Jerusalem.

Pauline Christianity

Pauline Christianity is attested as early as the year 49 when he wrote to Christians in Macedonia, commending their belief in the resurrection (1 Thess. 1:10).[28] Indeed, in each of the *Hauptebriefe*, Paul stated his own belief in Jesus' resurrection (Gal. 1:1; 1 Cor. 15:3–4; 2 Cor. 4:14; Phil. 3:10), a belief he likely held until the end of his life ca. 64 (cf. Rom. 10:9).[29] However, Pauline Christianity was also a breakaway movement inasmuch as it abandoned certain practices that the initial movement embraced due to it being thoroughly Jewish. Thus, despite one Jesus tradition claiming kingdom entrance is dependent upon a person's faithfulness to Torah (Matt. 5:18–20), a significant evolution occurred as Pauline Christianity abandoned strict compliance to the Mosaic law. He no longer required circumcision (Gal. 2:3; 1 Cor. 7:18) and even discouraged its practice (Gal. 5:2). Similarly, Paul did not enforce Jewish dietary restrictions (Rom. 14), nor did he forbid table fellowship between Jews and Gentiles (Gal. 1:11–14). In general, he did not encourage strict devotion to Torah for either his own Gentile followers (Gal. 3) or for those Gentiles who had become Christians under the leadership of others, such as Roman Christians (Rom. 3–4). From this distinctive feature, Ehrman observes,

---

[24] Rodney Stark, *The Triumph of Christianity: How the Jesus Movement Became the World's Largest Religion* (New York: HarperOne, 2011), 179–82.

[25] Bart D. Ehrman, *The Triumph of Christianity: How a Forbidden Religion Swept the World* (New York: Simon and Schuster, 2018), 69.

[26] See also, Pritz, *Nazarene Jewish Christianity*, 122–27.

[27] Eve, *Behind the Gospels*, 168.

[28] Ehrman, *Did Jesus Exist?*, 117-18.

[29] Cf. Bart D. Ehrman, *Forged: Writing in the Name of God—Why the Bible's Authors Are Not Who We Think They Are* (New York: HarperOne, 2011), 93 and Edward Champlin, *Nero* (Cambridge, MA: Harvard University Press, 2003), 121–22.

Thus, to be members of God's covenantal people, it was not necessary for gentiles to become Jews. They did not need to be circumcised, observe the Sabbath, keep kosher, or follow any of the other prescriptions of the law. They needed only to believe in the death and resurrection of the messiah Jesus. This was an earth-shattering realization for Paul. Prior to this, the followers of Jesus—the first Christians—were of course Jews who understood that he was the messiah who had died and been raised from the dead. But they knew this as the act of the Jewish god given to his people, the Jews. Certainly gentiles could find this salvation as well. But first they had to be Jewish. Not for Paul. Jew or gentile, it did not matter. What mattered was faith in Christ.[30]

Demographically, as with the initial movement, it is difficult to tell how many embraced Pauline Christianity, but during the years 40 and 100, when Pauline Christianity arose, Stark maintains that the number of Christians in the world increased from 1,000 to 7,434.[31] During the church's pre-Pauline period, the Christian religion experienced a growth rate of 24% per year, but that growth rate slowed to a rate of about 3% during the Pauline era of the first century.[32] According to Paul's Epistles, between the late 40s to about 100 CE, new churches appeared in cities across the Roman Empire while Pauline Christianity likely competed with other Christianities throughout Syria, Asia Minor, Cyprus, Macedonia, Achaia, and Rome.[33]

In summary, the Pauline version of Christianity made its appearance, at the latest, around the year 49 and possibly earlier. This second form of Christianity possibly retained some of the christological features of the earliest oral traditions and passed on the belief that Jesus rose from the dead. However, in some areas of practice, Pauline Christianity differed from the initial movement, at least as far as its Gentile population was concerned. It forsook circumcision, the Jewish dietary restrictions, and strict obedience to the Mosaic law. The period during which Pauline Christianity flourished saw a slowing in the growth rate of Christianity as compared to the period preceding it, but an increase in the number of churches. Pauline Christianity probably wielded influence from Syria, across Asia Minor, and as far west as Rome. In time, a third major form of Christianity broke from the original oral traditions.

Ebionite Christianity

This section describes a form of Jewish Christianity that has come to be known as "Ebionism."[34] The earliest explicit witness to Ebionite Christianity comes from Irenæus in the second century.[35] According to him, the Ebionites rejected Pauline Christianity, denied the virgin birth of Jesus, and subscribed to only Matthew's Gospel (*Haer.* 1.26.1–2). However,

---

[30] Ehrman, *The Triumph of Christianity*, 80.

[31] Stark, *The Triumph of Christianity*, 183.

[32] These numbers assume Christianity began the year Jesus died per Ehrman's estimation (i.e. 30 CE), and that Stark is correct about the initial group of Christians consisting of 120 persons, growing to 1000 by the year 40.

[33] Rodney Stark, *Cities of God: The Real Story of How Christianity Became an Urban Movement and Conquered Rome* (New York: HarperCollins, 2006), 43–65; Stark, *The Triumph of Christianity*, 186.

[34] Petri Luomanen, *Recovering Jewish-Christian Sects and Gospels* (Leiden, Netherlands: Brill, 2012), 17–49, 161–65, 233, https://doi.org/10.1163/9789004217430. There probably exists another grouping within Ebionism known as the Symmachians. Here, Ambrosiaster's description of the Symmachians matches other patristic characterizations of the Ebionites (*Comm. Gal.* Prologue), and even Eusebius states that Symmachus was himself an Ebionite (*Hist. eccl.* 6.17). See also A. F. J. Klijn and G. J. Reinink, *Patristic Evidence for Jewish-Christian Sects* (Leiden, Netherlands: Brill, 1973), 54, https://doi.org/10.1163/9789004268401.

[35] Klijn and Reinink, *Patristic Evidence*, 68.

Epiphanius testified in the fourth century that the Ebionites used a *Gospel of the Ebionites* which appears to be a "harmonization" of the Synoptic Gospels (*Pan.* 30).[36] He also reported that their edition of Matthew was retracted, leaving out the virgin birth narrative (30.13–14).[37] Epiphanius informed his readers that the Ebionites took their anti-Pauline stance due to the apostle's rejection of circumcision (30.16).

With regard to Ebionite Christology, Irenæus reported the Ebionites believed "Christ departed from Jesus, and that then Jesus suffered and rose again" (*Haer.* 3.21.1).[38] In other words, according to the earliest account of Ebionite Christology, it appears they believed only the *man* Jesus suffered on the cross while the Christ spirit departed Jesus prior to his crucifixion. In this way, Ebionite Christology differed from what Paul had preached, "that *Christ* died" (1 Cor. 15:3; emphasis added). While there are indications that Paul believed in Jesus as the pre-existent Son of God, whose being was placed into a woman (1 Cor. 10:4, 15:47; Gal. 4:4; Rom. 8:3), Ehrman concludes, "the Ebionites saw Jesus as completely human and not divine."[39]

Moreover, while Paul indicated there was discord between him and some unnamed individuals who disagreed with his anti-circumcision doctrine (Gal. 2:4–5), Paul also argued that he had received endorsement from the leaders of the Jerusalem church (vv. 7–9). Not surprisingly, then, Irenæus reports that the Ebionites "repudiate the Apostle Paul, maintaining that he was an apostate from the law" (*Haer.* 1.26.2). This may serve as the reason why, according to Origen (*Cels.* 5.65), the Ebionites rejected the Pauline Epistles, and it may also be their motive, according to Epiphanius (*Pan.* 30.16), for making false accusations against Paul.

The question of when Ebionite Christianity first manifested remains difficult to answer with precision. Petri Luomanen suggests the possibility that Ebionite Christianity formed when Christians fled from Jerusalem in the wake of Paul's persecution (Acts 8) and began to proselytize in Samaria, but this suggestion is based on tenuous inferences, and even Luomanen implies it is speculative at best.[40] The question then becomes, what is the *most likely* date of the Ebionite movement's inception in relation to the initial Christian movement and subsequent Pauline Christianity? One may be able to infer a possible date based on the following four points. First, according to Epiphanius, the Ebionites did not come into existence as a group until after the fall of Jerusalem (70 CE) when they supposedly separated themselves from the group of Jews that had fled to Pella (*Pan.* 30.2.7).[41] While this testimony is late, it is the only explicit reference

---

[36] See Ehrman, *Lost Christianities*, xi, 102. Petri Luomanen believes Epiphanius's report, while not primarily interested in historical facts, serves as "the richest ancient source on the Ebionites available" (Luomanen, *Recovering Jewish-Christian Sects*, 31).

[37] Ehrman, *Lost Christianities*, 109.

[38] Luomanen discusses the textual issues in Irenæus' statement and concludes that he intended to mean, "Ebionites . . . separated Christ and Jesus" (Luomanen, *Recovering Jewish-Christian Sects*, 19–20).

[39] Ehrman, *Lost Christianities*, 109; Larry Hurtado observes, "Though scholarly majorities can sometimes be wrong, we should note that the overwhelming majority of scholars in the field agree that there are at least a few passages in Paul's undisputed letters that reflect and presuppose the idea of Jesus' preexistence" (Larry W. Hurtado, *Lord Jesus Christ: Devotion to Jesus in Earliest Christianity* [Grand Rapids, MI: William B. Eerdmans Publishing Company, 2003], 119).

[40] Luomanen, *Recovering Jewish-Christian Sects*, 161–65.

[41] A. F. J. Klijn and G. J. Reinink believe that Epiphanius wanted to show that the Ebionites stemmed from Jewish Christians who had lived in Jerusalem (Klijn and Reinink, *Patristic Evidence*, 29).

regarding the formation of Ebionism. Pritz places the movement about thirty-years later. He maintains a difference between the Nazarenes and the Ebionites:

> The Nazarenes were distinct from the Ebionites and prior to them. In fact, we have found that it is possible that there was a split in Nazarene ranks around the turn of the first century. This split was either over a matter of christological doctrine or over leadership of the community. Out of this split came the Ebionites, who can scarcely be separated from the Nazarenes on the basis of geography, but who can be easily distinguished from the standpoint of Christology.[42]

Second, the Ebionite use of a harmonized Gospel text indicates the movement was in ascension after the Gospel of Mark had been written (ca. 70).[43] Third, the Ebionite's anti-Pauline stance suggests that Pauline Christianity already had time to circulate toward the end of the first century. Ehrman surmises that Ebionism may have developed after Paul's Galatian detractors had passed off the scene.[44] Finally, though admittedly an *argumentum ex silentio*, no mention is made among the church fathers until Irenæus in the second century. First century fathers, such as Polycarp and Papias who, like Irenæus, came from Asia Minor, make no mention of the Ebionites. While admittedly a *terminus a quo* for Ebionite Christianity cannot be established with certainty, the above points, when taken together, suggest that the movement probably did not begin until after the year 70, approximately twenty-years after Pauline Christianity first formed, despite the Ebionites claiming to have descended from the original Jewish leaders of the Jerusalem church, Peter and James.[45]

With regard to issues of Christian demography, as with the previous two forms of Christianity, knowing how many embraced Ebionism is nearly impossible. Nor is it possible to know how many churches (or synagogues), if any, wholly embraced Ebionism, though it is likely they were influential in Asia Minor, Rome, Alexandria, Judaea, Arabia Petraea, and Cyprus.[46] In summary, Ebionite Christianity may have developed at the end of the first century but most likely flourished in the second century. Ebionism was clearly distinct from Pauline Christology and retained strict compliance to the Mosaic law, including dietary restrictions, circumcision, and Sabbath observance. During this time period, the Christian population increased from 2,730 to 7,434 just as Ebionism and other Christianities spread throughout Asia Minor.[47]

Conclusion

Of course, there were other first century groups that fall under the rubric of Christianity.[48] However, the two detailed in this article were likely the first to materialize into

---

[42] Pritz, *Nazarene Jewish Christianity*, 108. Cf. Darren M. Slade, "*Arabia Haeresium Ferax* (Arabia Bearer of Heresies): Schismatic Christianity's Potential Influence on Muhammad and the Qur'an," *American Theological Inquiry* 7, no. 1 (January 2014): 50–51.

[43] Cf. Donatien de Bruyne, "Les plus anciens prologues latins des Evangiles," *Revue bénédictine* 40 (1928): 193–214, https://doi.org/10.1484/j.rb.4.03052; Ehrman, *Forged*, 71; and *Did Jesus Exist?*, 74–75.

[44] Ehrman, *Lost Christianities*, 100.

[45] Ibid.

[46] Cf. Irenæus, *Haer.* 3.21.1; Hippolytus, *Haer.* 7.22; Origen, *Cels.* 2.1; Eusebius, *Hist. eccl.* 3.27; Epiphanius, *Pan.* 30.2.7; 30.18.1; 40.1.3.

[47] Stark, *The Triumph of Christianity*, 183.

[48] These include the teachings of Cerinthus, the Balaamites, and the Nicolaitans.

significant movements. What this article has argued is that the initial movement of Christianity was the movement persecuted by Paul, and that by the end of the first century, two main schisms occurred, namely the Pauline and Ebionite movements. Of these two, Pauline Christianity arose before the Ebionism. Significantly, though, both movements found reception in several of the same regions, particularly Asia Minor.

In relation to Howard's "religion singularity," the implication of first century Christian diversity is that divergent belief systems tend to thrive among geographical melting pots. Hence, something like a present-day Asia Minor may help explain why the explosion of Christian denominations has reached a point of no return. Just as Asia Minor appears to have been a geographic conduit for diverse religious ideas in the first and second centuries, so too does the internet act as a similar conduit for diversity today. Coinciding with the proliferation of the internet, there has been a tendency toward religious pluralism and divergent theologies across the globe as people have access to more information with less external control.[49] If Asia Minor was a melting pot of diverse ideas, then it makes sense that competing forms of Christianities would exist in the same region. Likewise, if the internet is a melting pot of ideas today, then it makes sense that competing denominations would continue increasing. Of course, the internet was not responsible for the "religion singularity" since the phenomenon had already manifested decades before its invention. Rather than slow down, however, the internet may have aggravated the situation by allowing multiple divergent Christianities to exist unhindered in the same (cyber)space, just like Asia Minor did in the first and second centuries.

BIBLIOGRAPHY

Bauer, Walter. *Rechtgläubigkeit Und Ketzerei Im Ältesten Christentum* [Orthodoxy and Heresy in Earliest Christianity]. 2nd ed. Edited by Georg Strecker. Beiträge zur Historischen Theologie 10. Tübingen, Germany: Mohr (Siebeck), 1963.

Champlin, Edward. *Nero*. Cambridge, MA: Harvard University Press, 2003.

de Bruyne, Donatien. "Les plus anciens prologues latins des Evangiles." *Revue bénédictine* 40 (1928): 193–214. https://doi.org/10.1484/j.rb.4.03052.

Ehrman, Bart D. *Did Jesus Exist? The Historical Argument for Jesus of Nazareth*. 2012. Pbk. ed. Reprint, New York: HarperOne, 2013.

———. *Forged: Writing in the Name of God—Why the Bible's Authors Are Not Who We Think They Are* (New York: HarperOne, 2011).

———. *Lost Christianities: The Battle for Scripture and the Faiths We Never Knew*. New York: Oxford University Press, 2003.

———. *The Triumph of Christianity: How a Forbidden Religion Swept the World*. New York: Simon and Schuster, 2018.

Eve, Eric. *Behind the Gospels: Understanding the Oral Tradition*. 2013. Reprint, Minneapolis, MN: Fortress Press, 2014.

Ferguson, Everett, ed. "Volume Introduction." In *Doctrinal Diversity: Varieties of Early Christianity*. Recent Studies in Early Christianity 4, ix–xii. New York: Garland Publishing, 1999.

Hengel, Martin. *Between Jesus and Paul: Studies in the Earliest History of Christianity*. Translated by John Bowden. Philadelphia, PA: Fortress Press, 1983.

---

[49] See Jean-François Lyotard, *The Postmodern Condition: A Report on Knowledge*, trans. Geoff Bennington and Brian Massumi (1979; repr., Minneapolis, MN: University of Minnesota Press, 1984).

Howard, Kenneth W. *Paradoxy: Creating Christian Community Beyond Us and Them*. Brewster, MA: Paraclete Press, 2010.

———. "The Religion Singularity: A Demographic Crisis Destabilizing and Transforming Institutional Christianity." *International Journal of Religion and Spirituality in Society* 7, no. 2 (2017): 77–93. http://dx.doi.org/10.18848/2154-8633/cgp/v07i02/77-93.

Hultgren, Arland J. *The Rise of Normative Christianity*. Minneapolis, MN: Fortress Press, 1994.

Hurtado, Larry W. *Lord Jesus Christ: Devotion to Jesus in Earliest Christianity*. Grand Rapids, MI: William B. Eerdmans Publishing Company, 2003.

Kelly, J. N. D. *Early Christian Creeds*. 1950. 3rd ed. Reprint, New York: Continuum International Publishing Group, 2011. https://doi.org/10.4324/9781315836720.

Klijn, A. F. J., and G. J. Reinink. *Patristic Evidence for Jewish-Christian Sects*. Leiden, Netherlands: Brill, 1973. https://doi.org/10.1163/9789004268401.

Luomanen, Petri. *Recovering Jewish-Christian Sects and Gospels*. Leiden, Netherlands: Brill, 2012. https://doi.org/10.1163/9789004217430.

Lyotard, Jean-François. *The Postmodern Condition: A Report on Knowledge*. 1979. Translated by Geoff Bennington and Brian Massumi. Reprint, Minneapolis, MN: University of Minnesota Press, 1984.

Pritz, Ray A. *Nazarene Jewish Christianity: From the End of the New Testament Period Until Its Disappearance in the Fourth Century*. Leiden, Netherlands: Brill, 1988.

Slade, Darren M. "*Arabia Haeresium Ferax* (Arabia Bearer of Heresies): Schismatic Christianity's Potential Influence On Muhammad and the Qur'an." *American Theological Inquiry* 7, no. 1 (January 2014): 43–53.

Stark, Rodney. *Cities of God: The Real Story of How Christianity Became an Urban Movement and Conquered Rome*. New York: HarperCollins, 2006.

———. *The Triumph of Christianity: How the Jesus Movement Became the World's Largest Religion*. New York: HarperOne, 2011.

ABOUT THE AUTHOR

John F. Lingelbach holds an M.A.R. and M.Div. in Biblical Studies from Liberty University. He is currently a Ph.D. candidate in theology and apologetics. He is also an adjunct professor at Grace Christian University where he teaches Old and New Testament Survey.

SHERM 1/1 (2019): 21–28

A Cultural Cognition Perspective on Religion Singularity: How Political Identity Influences Religious Affiliation

A Position Paper by

Kevin S. Seybold,
Grove City College

Editor's Note: The "Position Paper" is a unique feature to SHERM journal where hand-selected scholars are invited to write their particular standpoint or attitude on a specific issue. The position paper is intended to engender support for the paper's argument. However, in contrast to a simple op-ed piece, the academic nature of this position paper derives its argumentation from facts, verifiable data, and/or the author's training and experience as a scholar in a particular field of study.

In this case, the author was asked to answer the following question: Assuming the "religion singularity" phenomenon is, in fact, occurring in institutional Christianity today, what do you believe is the primary cause(s) for this phenomenon's occurrence?

Abstract: Kenneth Howard argues in his paper, "The Religion Singularity," that institutional Christianity has experienced and will continue to experience an increase in the number of denominations and individual worship centers, which, along with a slower increase in the number of Christians in the US, will make institutional Christianity unsustainable in its current form. While there are, no doubt, many reasons why this religion singularity has or will take place, this paper examines the role of cultural cognition on the trends reported in Howard's article. Cultural commitments and values, such as group membership and identity, influence the position individuals take on a variety of religious and political topics, which can then lead to polarization on these issues within the broader society. While we might expect that religious affiliations play an important role in determining a person's political views, this article seeks to identify whether the reverse is also true, namely the extent to which political views affect an individual's religious affiliation. This article reviews research that suggests the increasing political polarization in the United States over the past few decades has contributed, along with other factors, to the religion singularity reported by Howard.

Keywords: Cultural Cognition, Religion Singularity, Politics, Group Identity, Ideology, Polarization

---

KENNETH HOWARD'S ARTICLE ON the "religion singularity" describes demographic trends that he argues will make "institutional Christianity unsustainable in its current forms."[1] These trends include a rapid increase in the number of denominations and individual worship centers along with a steady but slower increase in the number of Christians globally. A religion singularity occurred once the increase in worship centers and denominations exceeded the increase in number of new Christians. Howard argues that, along with the rising number of "nones" and religiously unaffiliated in the United States, this differential will drive the congregational size of denominations and worship centers down to potentially unsustainable levels by the end of the

---

[1] Kenneth W. Howard, "The Religion Singularity: A Demographic Crisis Destabilizing and Transforming Institutional Christianity," *International Journal of Religion and Spirituality in Society* 7, no. 2 (2017): 90, http://dx.doi.org/10.18848/2154-8633/cgp/v07i02/77-93.

Socio-Historical Examination of Religion and Ministry
Volume 1, Issue 1, Spring 2019 www.shermjournal.org
© Wipf and Stock Publishers. All Rights Reserved.
Permissions: shermeditor@gmail.com
ISSN 2637-7519 (print), ISSN 2637-7500 (online)
https://doi.org/10.33929/sherm.2019.vol1.no1.03 (article)

WIPF *and*
STOCK
Publishers

twenty-first century.[2] According to Howard's analysis of the data, institutional Christianity will have to adjust if it expects to survive in a healthy form in the years to come.

If Howard is accurate and a religion singularity has occurred (or will soon take place), what might account for these patterns that threaten institutional Christianity? Specifically, why was there such an increase in denominational fragmentation, from 9,300 to 34,200 (according to Howard's data) during the second half of the twentieth century?[3] In the social sciences, there frequently exists many potential causes for a particular phenomenon, and there are likely several factors driving the singularity trend Howard identifies. The purpose of this position paper is to examine the religion singularity from the perspective of cultural cognition, which refers to processes whereby cultural commitments and values (e.g. group membership and identity) influences the position a person adopts on a particular issue, such as gun control, climate change, same-sex marriage, etc. These cultural commitments act as a type of heuristic framework through which individuals assess data in order to form their opinions. In the context of religion singularity, perhaps growth in the number of denominations and worship centers over the past few decades is attributable to the increased political and religious polarization of the US population. We can conceptualize denominations and worship centers as social institutions that provide an individual with a sense of social identity. If people are making decisions about which religious group they will join on the basis of political (as well as religious) orientation, then the fragmentation and increasing number of denominations and centers of worship might actually reflect the increasing political polarization found in the United States. In other words, religious sorting occurs because partisans may select into politically like-minded social groups.[4]

Many factors can contribute to our sense of group identity, such as national, ethnic, and religious groups.[5] As social beings, humans need to affiliate with others for survival. Over the course of human history, the size of these groups has increased from small hunter-gathering groups to large nation states. Our minds evolved, in part, to facilitate the formation and maintenance of tribal in-groups; our brains are built for tribal life.[6] Certain cognitive processes function to differentiate the in-group ("us") from the out-group ("them"). As a result, we tend to accept the reliability of new information only if it is consistent with what we already believe to be true (a "biased assimilation" or "confirmation bias"). We also view beliefs held by our in-group as being objective and correct while beliefs held by out-groups as biased and erroneous ("naïve realism"), and we automatically dismiss evidence presented by the out-group before fully considering it ("reactive devaluation"). These biases in information processing are examples of motivated reasoning or cognition—the tendency of individuals to conform their evaluation of data in order to remain consistent with a stated goal or purpose that is oftentimes unrelated to factual accuracy.[7] Regularly, that goal or purpose is to be consistent with the thinking of the in-group.

---

[2] Howard, "The Religion Singularity," 77.

[3] Ibid., 82.

[4] Michele F. Margolis, *From Politics to the Pews How Partisanship and the Political Environment Shape Religious Identity* (Chicago, IL: The University of Chicago Press, 2018), 200, https://doi.org/10.7208/chicago/9780226555812.001.0001.

[5] Andrew L. Whitehead and Christopher P. Scheitle, "We the (Christian) People: Christianity and American Identity from 1996 to 2014," *Social Currents* 5, no. 2 (2018): 157–72, http://dx.doi.org/10.1177/2329496517725333.

[6] Joshua D. Greene, *Moral Tribes: Emotion, Reason, and the Gap Between Us and Them* (New York: Penguin Books, 2013), 69.

[7] Kevin S. Seybold, *Questions in the Psychology of Religion* (Eugene, OR: Cascade Books, 2017), 175.

Religious denominations or worship centers can function as an in-group for its members.[8] We might expect that religion plays an important role in determining a person's views on the political issues of the day, even influencing an individual's choice of membership in a particular political party. Hence, the religious group I belong to (my denomination and/or worship center) might affect the political party with which I affiliate. Indeed, religion trails only race as an indicator of political partisanship.[9] However, does a person's political identification affect an individual's religious affiliation, as well? Paul Djupe and his colleagues provide evidence for politics influencing religious association in their studies on the relationship between politics and religious disaffiliation.[10] These authors found that when political and religious identities are at odds with each other, politics (not religion) wins out. If congregants disagree with their church's position on a political issue (e.g. LGBTQ rights) and this issue becomes salient within the entire congregation (i.e. church leadership takes a position on the issue), then congregants are more likely to leave the religious organization, especially if they only marginally identify with the religious organization.[11] Political involvement of churches can, therefore, precipitate the loss of members when those members disagree with the congregational leadership as a whole.

In one of the first studies to investigate the role that politics plays in religious affiliation, Michael Hout and Claude Fischer found that the religiously tinged politics of the 1990s contributed to politically moderate and liberal congregants abandoning their religious attachments.[12] The authors argue that this is one factor that has contributed to the 30-year rise of the religiously unaffiliated ("nones"), which now comprises about 25% of the US population, according to recent surveys.[13] These "nones" are typically not atheists or secularists. What defines them is their "avoidance of churches" where they choose a religious affiliation (or lack thereof), at least in part, on the basis of their political views.[14] Stratos Patrikios also found that some religious believers modify their church attendance because of politics. Religiosity, according to Patrikios, is an unstable choice for many individuals, and this choice is open to

---

[8] Darren M. Slade, "Religious Homophily and Biblicism: A Theory of Conservative Church Fragmentation," *The International Journal of Religion and Spirituality in Society* 9, no. 1 (2019): 13–28, http://dx.doi.org/10.18848/2154-8633/cgp/v09i01/13-28.

[9] Margolis, *From Politics to the Pews*, 22.

[10] Paul A. Djupe, Jacob R. Neiheisel, and Kimberly H. Conger, "Are the Politics of the Christian Right Linked to State Rates of the Nonreligious? The Importance of Salient Controversy," *Political Research Quarterly* 71, no. 4 (2018): 910–22, http://dx.doi.org/10.1177/1065912918771526; Paul A. Djupe, Jacob R. Neiheisel, and Anand E. Sokhey, "Reconsidering the Role of Politics in Leaving Religion: The Importance of Affiliation," *American Journal of Political Science* 62, no. 1 (2018): 161–75, http://dx.doi.org/10.1111/ajps.12308.

[11] Landon Schnabel and Sean Bock, "The Persistent and Exceptional Intensity of American Religion: A Response to Recent Research," *Sociological Science* 4 (November 2017): 697, http://dx.doi.org/10.15195/v4.a28; Djupe, Neiheisel, and Conger, "Are the Politics of the Christian Right Linked," 910–22; Djupe, Neiheisel, and Sokhey, "Reconsidering the Role of Politics in Leaving Religion," 161–75.

[12] Michael Hout and Claude S. Fischer, "Why More Americans Have No Religious Preference: Politics and Generations," *American Sociological Review* 67, no. 2 (April 2002): 179, http://dx.doi.org/10.2307/3088891.

[13] Cf. Robert P. Jones et al., *Exodus: Why Americans are Leaving Religion—and Why They're Unlikely to Come Back* (Washington, DC: Public Religion Research Institute, 2016), 2, https://www.prri.org/wp-content/uploads/2016/09/PRRI-RNS-Unaffiliated-Report.pdf.

[14] Hout and Fischer, "Why More Americans Have No Religious Preference," 175.

secular influences, including those of a political nature.[15] Ultimately, political party identification provides a strong sense of belonging to a social in-group, and the ideology and partisanship within the party "may be able to 'construct' religious communities, by boosting movement within and perhaps eventually across these communities."[16] Political factors, consequently, might contribute to the rapid growth in the number of denominations and worship centers as documented by Howard.[17] Patrikios summarizes his findings, "Worshiping in a theologically conservative church seems to eventually function – at least in part – as a symbolic expression of conservatism and Republican partisanship." He speculates further, "The long-term consequence of this political religion could lead to an ideological and partisan sorting-out within politicized churches."[18]

Are the worship centers discussed in Howard's article politicized? Howard does acknowledge that megachurches are more likely to be conservative than progressive by which he probably means they are more likely *theologically* conservative.[19] Barney Warf and Morton Winsberg point out that megachurches tend to be located in small Southern counties where a large percentage of the population already attends church. Although often surrounded by more Democratic metropolitan regions, these counties tend to be politically conservative. Warf and Winsberg postulate a bi-directional association between megachurches and their political environment, whereby voting patterns are influenced by the conservative political perspectives found in these megachurches.[20] While not a direct measurement of political influence on religious affiliation, Warf and Winsberg's analysis of megachurch geographies is consistent with the proposal that people's political identity influences their religious choices—first, whether to attend church at all; and second, if attending, which religious group to join.

Michele Margolis in her recent book, *From Politics to the Pews*, provides longitudinal data to support her thesis that political motivations drive religious belief, behavior, and belonging.[21] Here, the term "God gap" is used to describe the fact that the more devoutly religious tend to belong to the Republican Party while the less devout are Democrats. This trend began in the 1970s and 1980s and continues today, exemplified by the white evangelical voting bloc. Why is there a close connection between religiosity and political membership? Conventional wisdom suggests that Americans rely on their religious identities to form their political judgments; they align their political identities with their preexisting religious identities.[22] However, Margolis argues that people also align their religious involvement with their political perspectives. In other words, political partisans select into or out of religious communities based on their political outlook. They find themselves, therefore, in "politically homogeneous social networks."[23] Once embedded in these homogeneous in-groups, they are exposed only to political views (as well as theological perspectives) that are consistent with the in-group. Thus, the church becomes a type of echo chamber "populated by like-minded

---

[15] Stratos Patrikios, "American Republican Religion? Disentangling the Causal Link Between Religion and Politics in the Us," *Political Behavior* 30, no. 3 (2008): 371, http://dx.doi.org/10.1007/s11109-008-9053-1.

[16] Ibid., 386.

[17] Howard, "The Religion Singularity," 77–93.

[18] Patrikios, "American Republican Religion?," 386.

[19] Howard, "The Religion Singularity," 89.

[20] Barney Warf and Morton Winsberg, "Geographies of Megachurches in the United States," *Journal of Cultural Geography* 27, no. 1 (2010): 42, http://dx.doi.org/10.1080/08873631003593216.

[21] Margolis, *From Politics to the Pews*.

[22] Ibid., 35–37.

[23] Ibid., 6.

partisans."[24] While this homogeneity increases the bond within a group, it can also foster political and religious animosity toward the "other" (i.e. those not part of the in-group).[25]

How might this alignment of religious identity with political identity look developmentally? When might this alignment take place? To answer this question, Margolis utilizes a life-cycle theory of religion. Here, religion is typically a peripheral concern for adolescents and young adults, but other aspects of identity, such as political outlook, become much more salient during these years. When adults begin to reconsider their religious involvement, generally once they have school-aged children living at home, their religious affiliation (or disaffiliation) is driven by their already established political identifications. The longitudinal data provided by Margolis support this hypothesis. Political partisanship plays a role when religious engagement decisions are made during this portion of the religious life cycle. The empirical data show that religiosities between Republicans and Democrats diverged (the "God gap") once people had school-aged children at home.[26] Republicans tended to affiliate with a religious group and adopt a religious identity while Democrats generally did not.

All of these studies suggest that political and religious ideologies shape an individual's identity, and identity automatically leads to an "us" versus "them" differentiation. Mason argues that what "liberals" and "conservatives" dislike about each other is the "otherness" of one's identity opponent (the out-group), and it is this preference for one's in-group and dislike of the out-group that drives the polarization seen along political and religious lines in the US today.[27] The complex interplay of politics and religion is again shown in the results of a study by Whitehead and his colleagues, which found that voting behavior (in this case, voting for Donald Trump in the 2016 Presidential election) was a function of a variety of factors, including anti-Black prejudice, negative attitudes toward immigration, derogatory views of Islam, and white Christian Nationalism (which the authors define as a set of beliefs that link being an American with being a Christian). These Trump supporters also saw similarities between the United States and the nation of Israel in the Old Testament, which coincides with their strong defense of America's perceived Christian heritage. The authors found that while political conservativism, party affiliation, and evangelical Protestant religion were correlated with voting behavior, the more robust predictor was the related but distinct factor of white Christian Nationalism.[28]

Studies like these warn against causal oversimplification by attributing political behavior predominantly to religious affiliation. Many reasons might be given for the "religion singularity" trend noted in Howard's article. The role of cultural cognition discussed here is only one of many possibilities. Nevertheless, the implications of the religion singularity are significant and will lead, Howard proposes, to a transformation of institutional Christianity altogether. While the absolute number of Christians in the US continues to rise, that increase is

---

[24] Margolis, *From Politics to the Pews*, 6.

[25] Slade, "Religious Homophily and Biblicism," 13–28.

[26] Margolis, *From Politics to the Pews*, 99.

[27] Lilliana Mason, "Ideologues Without Issues: The Polarizing Consequences of Ideological Identities," *Public Opinion Quarterly* 82, no. S1 (2018): 880–85, http://dx.doi.org/10.1093/poq/nfy005.

[28] Andrew L. Whitehead, Samuel L. Perry, and Joseph O. Baker, "Make America Christian Again: Christian Nationalism and Voting for Donald Trump in the 2016 Presidential Election," *Sociology of Religion* 79, no. 2 (2018): 147–71, http://dx.doi.org/10.1093/socrel/srx070. See also, Brian D. McLaren, "Conditions for the Great Religion Singularity," *Socio-Historical Examination of Religion and Ministry* 1, no. 1 (Spring 2019): 40–49, https://doi.org/10.33929/sherm.2019.vol1.no1.05.

surpassed by the number of denominations and/or individual worship centers. Many factors no doubt influence the increasing number of worship centers in America. The literature reviewed in this paper suggests that among these factors is political partisanship. People affiliate with a particular denomination or worship center, in part, because of a perceived similarity between the individual's political identity and the political orientation of their congregation. People are selecting their religious identities on the basis of politics. As the United States has become more politically polarized over the past few decades, this polarization has likely contributed to the acceleration in denominational divisions and worship centers that make up the religion singularity. From the perspective of cultural cognition, group memberships and other cultural commitments influence the position a person takes on various issues. The work of Margolis and others described above suggests that it is often the cultural commitments of political membership and identity that influence religious perspectives and affiliations. If these authors' interpretation of the data is accurate, then the religion singularity and the rise in denominations and worship centers goes beyond religion *per se* to include other cultural forces, not the least of which is political partisanship.

BIBLIOGRAPHY

Djupe, Paul A., Jacob R. Neiheisel, and Anand E. Sokhey. "Reconsidering the Role of Politics in Leaving Religion: The Importance of Affiliation." *American Journal of Political Science* 62, no. 1 (2018): 161–75. http://dx.doi.org/10.1111/ajps.12308.

Djupe, Paul A., Jacob R. Neiheisel, and Kimberly H. Conger. "Are the Politics of the Christian Right Linked to State Rates of the Nonreligious? The Importance of Salient Controversy." *Political Research Quarterly* 71, no. 4 (2018): 910–22. http://dx.doi.org/10.1177/1065912918771526.

Greene, Joshua D. *Moral Tribes: Emotion, Reason, and the Gap Between Us and Them.* New York: Penguin Books, 2013.

Hout, Michael, and Claude S. Fischer. "Why More Americans Have No Religious Preference: Politics and Generations." *American Sociological Review* 67, no. 2 (April 2002): 165–90. http://dx.doi.org/10.2307/3088891.

Howard, Kenneth W. "The Religion Singularity: A Demographic Crisis Destabilizing and Transforming Institutional Christianity." *International Journal of Religion and Spirituality in Society* 7, no. 2 (2017): 77–93. http://dx.doi.org/10.18848/2154-8633/cgp/v07i02/77-93.

Jones, Robert P., Daniel Cox, Betsy Cooper, and Rachel Lienesch. *Exodus: Why Americans are Leaving Religion—and Why They're Unlikely to Come Back.* Washington, DC: Public Religion Research Institute, 2016. https://www.prri.org/wp-content/uploads/2016/09/PRRI-RNS-Unaffiliated-Report.pdf.

Margolis, Michele F. *From Politics to the Pews How Partisanship and the Political Environment Shape Religious Identity.* Chicago, IL: The University of Chicago Press, 2018. https://doi.org/10.7208/chicago/9780226555812.001.0001.

Mason, Lilliana. "Ideologues Without Issues: The Polarizing Consequences of Ideological Identities." *Public Opinion Quarterly* 82, no. S1 (2018): 866–87. http://dx.doi.org/10.1093/poq/nfy005.

McLaren, Brian D. "Conditions for the Great Religion Singularity." *Socio-Historical Examination of Religion and Ministry* 1, no. 1 (Spring 2019): 40–49, https://doi.org/10.33929/sherm.2019.vol1.no1.05.

Patrikios, Stratos. "American Republican Religion? Disentangling the Causal Link Between Religion and Politics in the Us." *Political Behavior* 30, no. 3 (2008): 367–89. http://dx.doi.org/10.1007/s11109-008-9053-1.

Schnabel, Landon, and Sean Bock. "The Persistent and Exceptional Intensity of American Religion: A Response to Recent Research." *Sociological Science* 4 (2017): 686–700. http://dx.doi.org/10.15195/v4.a28.

Seybold, Kevin S. *Questions in the Psychology of Religion*. Eugene, OR: Cascade Books, 2017.

Slade, Darren M. "Religious Homophily and Biblicism: A Theory of Conservative Church Fragmentation." *The International Journal of Religion and Spirituality in Society* 9, no. 1 (2019): 13–28. http://dx.doi.org/10.18848/2154-8633/cgp/v09i01/13-28.

Warf, Barney, and Morton Winsberg. "Geographies of Megachurches in the United States." *Journal of Cultural Geography* 27, no. 1 (2010): 33–51. http://dx.doi.org/10.1080/08873631003593216.

Whitehead, Andrew L., and Christopher P. Scheitle. "We the (Christian) People: Christianity and American Identity from 1996 to 2014." *Social Currents* 5, no. 2 (2018): 157–72. http://dx.doi.org/10.1177/2329496517725333.

Whitehead, Andrew L., Samuel L. Perry, and Joseph O. Baker. "Make America Christian Again: Christian Nationalism and Voting for Donald Trump in the 2016 Presidential Election." *Sociology of Religion* 79, no. 2 (2018): 147–71. http://dx.doi.org/10.1093/socrel/srx070.

ABOUT THE AUTHOR

Kevin S. Seybold is professor of psychology at Grove City College where he teaches courses in behavioral neuroscience, cognition, and the psychology of religion. A graduate of Greenville College (B.A.) and Marquette University (M.A.), he received his Ph.D. in physiological psychology from the University of Wisconsin-Milwaukee. Seybold has published articles in *Physiology & Behavior*, the *International Journal of Neuroscience, Biological Psychiatry, Current Directions in Psychological Science*, the *Journal of Behavioral Medicine*, and the *Journal of Psychology and Christianity* among others. He is the author of *Explorations in Neuroscience, Psychology and Religion* (2007) and *Questions in the Psychology of Religion* (2017).

MORE FROM THE AUTHOR

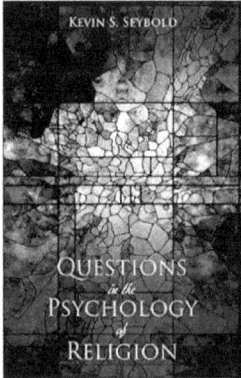

Questions in the Psychology of Religion
(2017, Cascade Books)

Kevin S. Seybold

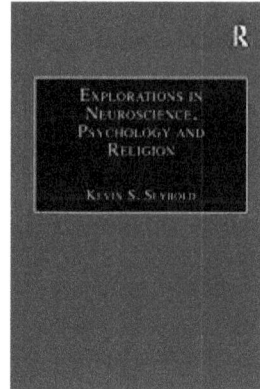

***Explorations in Neuroscience,
Psychology and Religion***
(2007, Routledge)

Kevin S. Seybold

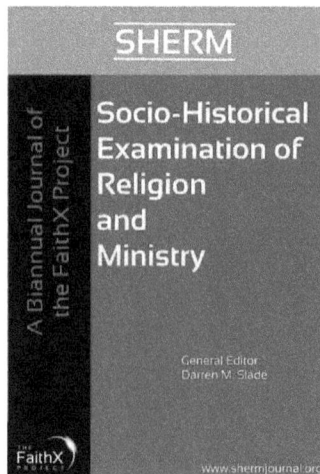

SHERM 1/1 (2019): 29–38

Is the Disintegration of Christianity a Problem— or Even a Surprise?

A Position Paper by

Jack David Eller,
Community College of Denver

Editor's Note: The "Position Paper" is a unique feature to SHERM journal where hand-selected scholars are invited to write their particular standpoint or attitude on a specific issue. The position paper is intended to engender support for the paper's argument. However, in contrast to a simple op-ed piece, the academic nature of this position paper derives its argumentation from facts, verifiable data, and/or the author's training and experience as a scholar in a particular field of study.

In this case, the author was asked to answer the following question: Assuming the "religion singularity" phenomenon is, in fact, occurring in institutional Christianity today, what do you believe is the primary cause(s) for this phenomenon's occurrence?

Abstract: This article argues that if Kenneth Howard's prediction of a "religion singularity" is true, it should not be a worry for social scientists, who must remain neutral on religious matters. Further, the deinstitutionalization, fragmentation, atomization, and even extinction of religion should come as no surprise to scholars who have observed these processes repeatedly. This process occurs not only in the realm of religion but in all social domains, from family and marriage to government—and indeed not only in social domains but in the natural world, as well. Contemporary forces of mediatization and neoliberalism are only the latest threats to institutional membership, creating a crisis among established authorities and encouraging "irregular" religion just as much as they encourage "irregular" employment. While the "religious economy" model suggests an adaptation of religion to the tastes and preferences of today's religious consumer, ethnographic evidence illustrates the difference between religious institutions and religiosity, the rise of multiple small religious movements, and the struggle for survival between sects, denominations, and churches. Ultimately it may be the case that the institutional phase of Christianity was only one moment in its religious evolution, which evolved from small, local, independent congregations and may return to—or end in—that form.

Keywords: deinstitutionalization, religious movement, religious economy, religious evolution, crisis of authority, religion singularity

WHEN I WAS DOING anthropological fieldwork in Australia in the late 1980s, I discovered a small Pentecostal outpost in the Aboriginal community of Yuendumu. When I say "small," I mean *five active members*, all of them young adult men, as well as two organizers from outside the community. Aside from its very (and unlikely) existence, the congregation was noteworthy in two ways. First, it was predictably plugged into global charismatic Christian movements; for instance, receiving literature and videos from Jimmy Swaggart's ministry. Second, it was understandably quite divisive among the Warlpiri residents of Yuendumu, many of whom were nominal Baptists due to the origin of the settlement as a Baptist mission. We might even say that this division was experienced as a "crisis," drawing members away from the dominant, virtually monopolistic Yuendumu Baptist church while driving wedges between kin.

Socio-Historical Examination of Religion and Ministry
Volume 1, Issue 1, Spring 2019 www.shermjournal.org
© Wipf and Stock Publishers. All Rights Reserved.
Permissions: shermeditor@gmail.com
ISSN 2637-7519 (print), ISSN 2637-7500 (online)
https://doi.org/10.33929/sherm.2019.vol1.no1.04 (article)

WIPF *and*
STOCK
Publishers

The situation in Yuendumu can perhaps be construed as a moment in the inexorable march toward Kenneth Howard's "religion singularity," as it posed a potential demographic calamity for, and threatened to destabilize and transform institutional (Baptist) Christianity in Warlpiri society. Anthropologists have long noted the proliferation of small, independent, and often decidedly unorthodox sects and churches. Some of these movements have striven for, and achieved to some degree, institutional (or what Howard calls "denominational") status, like the Presbyterian Church of Ghana. Most strikingly, this denomination launched an American branch, the Presbyterian Church of Ghana in New York (PCGNY) as an "overseas mission" with the goal "to propagate the message and mission of the Christian church in the United States through its own brand of Ghanaian presbyterianism [sic]"[1]—as if the United States was not already, or not sufficiently or correctly, Christian! On the other hand, David Martin notes that many Pentecostal and other Protestant congregations have the character of "local house groups and store-front churches" founded and operated by "religious entrepreneurs," some of whom endure while many store-fronts, if not most, do not.[2]

In the following short commentary, I do not intend to dispute Howard's conclusions or quibble with his math. It may well be that institutional Christianity is heading toward a "singularity" (not the term I would use), a vanishing point of dis-integration where each congregation has just one member. Nor will I be critiquing the truth-claims of any particular Christian sect or of Christianity as such. Whether Christianity—or more accurately, one version or another of Christianity—is true or false, or whether a supreme being is driving or allowing doctrinal and congregational proliferation, is quite irrelevant to the social fact of that proliferation. I will instead be making two general sociological points. First, as (ideally) neutral scholars, we cannot be alarmed about the "religion singularity." Our job is to watch, record, and explain; only partisans will take pleasure or pain in any particular outcome. Second, and more importantly, as informed observers of cultural processes, we should not be surprised by evolutionary changes—including critical or fatal changes—in the institutional structure of religion because such processes have been in effect since the dawn of religion and indeed are not restricted to religion or even to culture. It is purely evolution.

Howard writes with an urgent tone as he predicts the decline of institutional Christianity; although, it is not clear that the future of the religion "looking more like it did in the first century than at any time since: more diverse and less hierarchical, more faith than religion, and more a movement than an institution" is necessarily a bad thing.[3] After all, many Christian fundamentalists today and in the past aspired to return Christianity to its "primitive church" roots. As objective and nonpartisan chroniclers of religious change, we cannot indulge in angst. Yet, we can imagine that great distress was, indeed, felt by sixteenth century Catholics in the face of the Protestant onslaught, by ancient Romans as they lost ground to insurgent Christians, and by Jews who watched the early Jesus movement forever fracture "God's People" and the Nation of Israel.

And that is the real point that I want to make. Even if contemporary Christianity is in a state of profound transformation, there is nothing new happening here. At least since Martin

---

[1] Moses O. Biney, *From Africa to America: Religion and Adaptation among Ghanaian Immigrants in New York* (New York: NYU Press, 2011), 68, https://doi.org/10.18574/nyu/9780814786390.001.0001.

[2] David Martin, "Pentecostalism: An Alternative Form of Modernity and Modernization?" in *Global Pentecostalism in the 21st Century*, ed. Robert W. Hefner (Bloomington, IN: Indiana University Press, 2013), 37–62.

[3] Kenneth W. Howard, "The Religion Singularity: A Demographic Crisis Destabilizing and Transforming Institutional Christianity," *International Journal of Religion and Spirituality in Society* 7, no. 2 (2017): 90, http://dx.doi.org/10.18848/2154-8633/cgp/v07i02/77-93.

Luther tacked up his Ninety-Five Theses, Christianity has been in a constant state of decentralization and multiplication. Where there was once a single supposedly "catholic" church, there were now two, then three, then thousands. In fact, as anyone acquainted with Christian history must immediately grant, Christianity has never been centralized or fully institutionalized, regardless if we consider the early disagreements and controversies over Marcionism, Arianism, Docetism, *ad infinitum*; the Great Schism of Western and Eastern/Orthodox churches; or the manifold medieval heresies of the Cathars, the Waldensians, the Hussites, the Bogomils, and so forth.[4] Martin Luther merely broke the alleged monopoly of the Catholic Church once and for all.

Lutheranism opened the floodgate of protest movements with its insistence on "conscience" and *sola scriptura*, on which no consensus existed. "Every man his own priest" portends with centrifugal certainty to the evacuation of the center and, at its extreme, to the church-of-one. Protestantism was and remains the license to start a new "worship center" (in Howard's terminology) which may grow into a sect, a denomination, or even a religion. The process that Howard bemoans has been the regular state of Christianity for half a millennium; although, if he is right, it is reaching its logical end.

Not only is the fragmentation of institutional Christianity old and common by now, but the phenomenon is in no way unique to that religion. The unity of Judaism ended, if it ever existed, with the fall of the Temple. Without a central focal point of worship or a single professional priesthood, the synagogue tradition developed, with a myriad of local congregations led by rabbis and a number of general schools of Judaism including reform, liberal, and orthodox.[5] Islam split early into Sunni and Shia branches and is currently undergoing its own crisis of dissolution-through-multiplication as new movements, interpretations, and leaders splinter the *umma*. Entire new religions have burst from the shells of the old, including Sikhism and Baha'i. In the case of Islam—and probably with instructive value for other religions—the issue is not so much a crisis of demographics as a crisis of *authority* since, for example, the *'ulema* of Al-Azhar University no longer possess the sole authority to speak for the faith.[6] Traditional institutions and elites have lost control as religion, whether it is Islam, Christianity, or any other system, has become increasingly "popularized" in the sense of being "of, by, and for the people," who have understandably taken it in unprecedented directions. This evolution occurs much to the consternation of traditional religious leaders and experts, not to mention state elites who often attempt to promote, control, or coopt "official" religion in the service of the state.

Interestingly, a similar anxiety has gripped the atheist community in the United States where there was once perhaps a dream of a single unified organization and voice for the godless. For a moment, that voice was Madalyn Murray O'Hair and the organization was American

---

[4] On the divisions and disputes within early Christianity, see Walter Bauer, *Orthodoxy and Heresy in Earliest Christianity*, 2nd ed., ed. and trans. Robert A. Kraft and Gerhard Krodel (Philadelphia: Fortress Press, 1971) and James D. G. Dunn, *Unity and Diversity in the New Testament: An Inquiry into the Character of Earliest Christianity* (London: SCM Press, 1977).

[5] On the history of Judaism after the destruction of the second temple, see Solomon Grayzel, *A History of the Jews: From the Babylonian Exile to the Present* (New York: The New American Library, 1968).

[6] On the intellectual and institutional history of modern Islam, see for example, Albert Hourani, *Arabic Thought in the Liberal Age, 1798–1939* (New York: Oxford University Press, 1962), https://doi.org/10.1017/cbo9780511801990.

Atheists; but when Freedom from Religion Foundation broke away, the movement was cleft with further fissures in the form of Atheist Alliance International, Secular Student Alliance, Freethought Society, and so on and so forth, not to mention many local unaffiliated groups and movements. One might wonder, despite the documented growth of the atheist/agnostic/humanist/secularist/none/done category (and note how this population cannot even settle on a name!), whether it too is confronting a singularity of group expansion outpacing population growth.

Admittedly, the catastrophe may be more acute for institutional Christianity than for other religions (and non-religious aspects of culture) precisely because Christianity yearned for, and temporarily appeared to achieve, centralization on a scale that no other religion has accomplished. There is nothing like a Pope or Catholic Church in Judaism or Islam, let alone in Hinduism or Buddhism. This is not to say that there is no longing in other religions for unity, as in the Islamic vision of the caliphate; it is to say, however, that whatever unity they can reference is in the distant past or the remote future, if not the pure imagination (for instance, the *salafiyyah*, the "pious predecessors" or first generation of Muhammad's followers, playing the same role for Muslims that the primitive church plays for Christians). So, the dissolution of institutional Christianity no doubt feels more foreign and direr than it would with other religions. But, as we just established, the centralization and institutionalization of Christianity was always something of an ideal and an ideology rather than a fact.

This brings me to my fundamental point. Anthropology, as well as a close and honest study of religion in general, teaches us that religions (and the wider cultures within which they are set and into which they are integrated) are not eternal stable entities but are mobile, constructed, and *evolving* things like any natural species.[7] Moreover, the same general processes found in organic evolution also occur in sociocultural evolution. New forms emerge (speciation) and old forms disappear (extinction). In between, forms are continuously changing in adaptation to their environment, physical and social, or by sheer random mutation. Institutions, like Howard's "denominations," routinely shoot off new branches (every denomination *was* a new branch at one time), and they swap DNA with other religions, denominations, sects, and cults and with non-religious aspects of culture.[8] How else can we explain Mormonism, absorbing themes from American and Native American history into the overall Christian narrative, or "Heaven's Gate" (formally, TELAH or The Evolutionary Level Above Human), the suicide cult that mixed loosely Christian ideas with computer technology, ufology, and *Star Trek* (calling the previous and current alien landing parties among us "away teams")?[9]

So, the broad evolutionary processes of speciation, hybridization, and extinction are as normal in culture—and religion is nothing more than a domain of culture—as in nature. Christianity itself was obviously a bud off the stalk of Judaism; and as it developed over the centuries, it soaked up elements from Greco-Roman, Germanic and Nordic, and other cultures that it encountered. As the Ghanaian Presbyterian church illustrates, this evolutionary process is hardly finished and never will be. Indeed, Catholic authorities have explicitly recognized "inculturation" as a valid strategy for Christianity. Aylward Shorter, a Catholic "mission

---

[7] David Eller, "Christianity Evolving: On the Origin of Christian Species," in *The End of Christianity*, ed. John W. Loftus (Amherst, NY: Prometheus Books, 2011), 23–51.

[8] Cf. Darren M. Slade, "Religious Homophily and Biblicism: A Theory of Conservative Church Fragmentation," *The International Journal of Religion and Spirituality in Society* 9, no. 1 (2019): 13–28, http://dx.doi.org/10.18848/2154-8633/cgp/v09i01/13-28.

[9] See Jack David Eller, *Introducing Anthropology of Religion: Culture to the Ultimate*, 2nd ed. (New York: Routledge, 2015), https://doi.org/10.4324/9781315740157.

anthropologist," cites Pedro Arrupe's concept of inculturation in his book, *Toward a Theology of Inculturation*:

> the incarnation of Christian life and of the Christian message in a particular cultural context, in such a way that this experience not only finds expression through elements proper to the culture in question (this alone would be no more than a superficial adaptation) but becomes a principle that animates, directs, and unifies the culture, transforming it and remaking it so as to bring about a "new creation."[10]

As he added, this tactic implies "that the Christian message transforms a culture. It is also the case that Christianity is transformed by culture."[11]

This inculturation means that Christians and scholars can expressly expect—and the Catholic Church has actually encouraged—that local Christianities will vary. A case in point is the Aymara, an indigenous people of Bolivia, where Catholic missionaries aided the natives to find "a way of being Aymara the way that Jesus would have been Aymara"[12] and to go so far as to "to live and write their own Aymara New Testament."[13] Call it syncretism or hybridization, but inculturation is an invitation to add one more Christianity to the legion of Christianities.

As we also emphasized above, while such creativity has always been a live (although often heretical) possibility in Christianity, Protestantism legitimized it in a way from which there was no turning back. Protestantism is not an institution but a style or attitude, and that very non-institutional and anti-institutional spirit empowered individuals to start as many denominations, sects, and worship centers as they like. Granted, some Protestant movements have sought to re-impose a degree of institutional order, as in the Anglican Church or various Baptist conventions, but the schismatic cat has long been out of the bag, and there will never again be Christian unanimity or Lewisian "mere Christianity" (if there ever was unanimity).

Indeed, to extend our evolutionary analysis, we might consider the big, long-term institutions like the Catholic Church to be the exceptions in the evolutionary history of Christianity and of religion in general. As is well known, most religions lack any such institutional form (a few like Cao Dai in Vietnam have tried to emulate it), and even in the Christian context it may be better understood as one form among many. In fact, *institutional* Christianity appears to be more of a momentary aberration in the larger evolutionary development of religion than it has been *the* form or model of faith. Denominations in Howard's sense may then be the mega-fauna that roamed and ruled the earth for a time but, like all living things, were destined to come to an end and perhaps be replaced by humbler descendants. So— not to press the analogy too far—what we might be observing with the "religion singularity" is less a Permian Dying than a Cambrian Explosion of religion.

Another way to think about the problem that Howard identifies is Rodney Stark's "religious economy" model. Largely putting an economic façade on an evolutionary process, Stark recommended that we perceive religion as just another good that is produced, marketed,

---

[10] Cited in Aylward Shorter, *Toward a Theology of Inculturation* (Eugene, OR.: Wipf & Stock, 2006), 11.
[11] Ibid., 14.
[12] Andrew Orta, "Converting Difference: Metaculture, Missionaries, and the Politics of Locality," *Ethnology* 37, no. 2 (Spring 1998): 165–85, http://dx.doi.org/10.2307/3774002.
[13] Ibid., 172.

sold, bought, and consumed. In this scheme, religions and/or their constituent parts (churches, denominations, worship centers, etc.) are "firms" that offer a supply of religion to customers. Notwithstanding his questionable assumption that there is a constant demand for such products (the rise of religious Nones-and-Dones upsets that assumption), Stark maintained that the best kind of religious market was a *free* religious market, where each religious firm "caters to the special needs and tastes of specific market segments."[14] Note that Stark and his collaborators abandoned any hope of the return to a religious monopoly and truly believed that such a condition was stultifying to religion. Instead, it is beneficial to have many religions and many denominations, worship centers, etc. in a society. Their competition makes them try harder and offer better products (i.e. religious goods that people really want). On the other hand, when there is a single religion (often established and aided by the state) or when there is a regulated religious economy, religious firms get lazy, do not meet the needs of their customers, and generate lower levels of religiosity. People inevitably stop consuming, and the religion, denomination, or worship center goes out of business.

This Darwinian or Spencerian model of religion provides the mechanism by which religious species or populations (in the biological sense, of the local segment of a species) arise, change, and decline. We might add one more point about the environment in which contemporary religions must live, adapt, migrate, or die. No doubt, whether or not we subscribe to Stark's baldly economic view of things, religions (and their denominations and worship centers) must compete, not only with each other but with the mundane and profane facets of modern life, whether it be science, work, or Sunday football. Starting in the mid-twentieth century, this cultural environment became even more unconducive to institutional monopolies on religion. Beginning with radio and television transmissions of worship, and creating new religious celebrities like Bishop Fulton Sheen and Billy Graham and a new mode of televangelism, believers have been offered more (unconventional) ways to practice their faith. It is no surprise, then, that social media and the internet, with their tendencies toward do-it-yourself culture and interest/identity niches, have fostered deinstitutionalization and decongregationalization (i.e. allowing people to perform their religious duties apart from the dictates or confines of the institution).[15]

In fact, the deinstitutionalization of religion is just one part of a trend noted by sociologists and anthropologists toward a widespread retreat of institutions, from marriage to work.[16] Just as more people choose (or are forced into) "irregular employment" and "side hustles" to make a living, so too will more people choose irregular or side religion. Just as more people opt for living together outside of marriage (or living alone), so too will more people opt for believing together outside of denominations (or even believing alone). Indeed, under the conditions of postmodernism and neoliberalism, scholars have noted the collapse of "grand

---

[14] Rodney Stark and Laurence R. Iannaccone, "A Supply-Side Reinterpretation of the 'Secularization' of Europe," *Journal for the Scientific Study of Religion* 33, no. 3 (September 1994): 232, https://doi.org/10.2307/1386688.

[15] In the case of Islam, see Gary R. Bunt, *Hashtag Islam: How Cyber-Islamic Environments are Transforming Religious Authority* (Chapel Hill, NC: University of North Carolina Press, 2018).

[16] In the case of marriage, see Andrew J. Cherlin, "The Deinstitutionalization of American Marriage," *Journal of Marriage and Family* 66, no. 4 (2004): 848–61, http://dx.doi.org/10.1111/j.0022-2445.2004.00058.x.

narratives,"[17] as well as the decay of big government and the classic Weberian state.[18] We should only expect the collapse and decay of big religion, but these conditions have not meant the end of narratives or government or religion. Foucault diagnosed the diffusion of "governmentality" into more corners of society, and we might equally predict the diffusion of religiosity or religio-mentality, which tends to replace big religion with smaller specialized ones. One powerful conclusion is that the era of denominational institutions which Howard predicts was only a phase in the story of Christianity, suited for some social milieus but unsuited for today's social reality. From movement Christianity came, and to movement it may return.

Finally, is institutional Christianity doomed to pass away with a bang or with a whimper? The truth is that the proliferation of denominations, sects, and worship centers at the expense of institutions is not *less* religion but *more* religion. When a religious edifice is shattered, its countless shards may live on and prosper. This is a lesson that should have been learned from the successful navigation of the Protestant "crisis" in the 1500s: Christianity has emerged not weaker for the Reformation but stronger for it. I have made the same point to my atheist friends, who have despaired about the loss of consensus through the multiplication of atheist/secularist organizations. "Don't worry," I assure them, "having two or three or a dozen national and international organizations is not a bad thing, and the presence of small local atheist meetings—just like house churches and prayer groups, exploited so brilliantly by megachurches—actually allow atheism to reach more people and to adapt to more identities and interests." Call it target marketing.

Still, current experience teaches us that institutional religion is not the only kind of religion; "religion" is not synonymous with "institution." The Soviet Union learned the hard way that active suppression of church institutions could not and did not extinguish religiosity. As Gregory Freeze describes it, the crucial error of the Communist Party was to assume that Christianity equaled church institutions; from the regime's perspective, undermining the Orthodox Church and its authorities amounted to undermining religion. However, by attacking the institutional church, the Soviets only decentralized and popularized religion, in the literal sense of leaving it in the hands of the ordinary people. Freeze claims that the government "inadvertently empowered...the zealous activists who, for decades under the ancient regime, had been demanding more authority for the parish community."[19] No longer contained by the priesthood, Christianity became vernacularized in a new and sometimes frightening way: "displays of piety spilled over into the public arena—most dramatically, in an epidemic of 'miracles' and 'icon renewals' that occurred outside parish churches and triggered spontaneous mass pilgrimages."[20] In the end, Soviet actions "weakened the Church but strengthened the church."[21] That is, they weakened the institution but strengthened the faithful.

---

[17] Jean-François Lyotard, *The Postmodern Condition: A Report on Knowledge*, trans. Geoff Bennington and Brian Massumi (1979; repr., Minneapolis, MN: University of Minnesota Press, 1984).

[18] Rogers Brubaker and David D. Laitin, "Ethnic and Nationalist Violence," *Annual Review of Sociology* 24, no. 1 (1998): 423–52, http://dx.doi.org/10.1146/annurev.soc.24.1.423.

[19] Gregory L. Freeze, "Subversive Atheism: Soviet Antireligious Campaigns and the Religious Revival in Ukraine in the 1920s," in *State Secularism and Lived Religion in Soviet Russia and Ukraine*, ed. Catherine Wanner (New York: Oxford University Press, 2012), 31.

[20] Ibid., 40.

[21] Ibid., 34.

I think we can safely say, to paraphrase Mark Twain, that the reports of the death of Christianity are greatly exaggerated. More likely, if present trends continue with the "religion singularity," and if present cultural circumstances persist or intensify, the dinosaurs of church institutions (Howard's denominations) may perish, to be replaced by less-impressive successors like lizards and chickens. Indeed, there are more lizards and chickens today than there ever were dinosaurs. Future Christianity may look nothing like its familiar institutional form, but then that form looked nothing like its original form. And if institutional Christianity should become so atomized that it fades entirely into that good night, then it is nothing that objective scholars should celebrate or lament any more than the extinction of Druidism or Norse religion (both of which, incidentally, live on in various incarnations of neo-paganism). All things evolve, and all things pass: it is the natural (and cultural) order of the world.

BIBLIOGRAPHY

Bauer, Walter. *Orthodoxy and Heresy in Earliest Christianity*. 2nd ed. Edited and translated by Robert A. Kraft and Gerhard Krodel. Philadelphia: Fortress Press, 1971.

Biney, Moses O. *From Africa to America: Religion and Adaptation among Ghanaian Immigrants in New York*. New York: New York University Press, 2011. https://doi.org/10.18574/nyu/9780814786390.001.0001.

Brubaker, Rogers, and David D. Laitin. "Ethnic and Nationalist Violence." *Annual Review of Sociology* 24, no. 1 (1998): 423–52. http://dx.doi.org/10.1146/annurev.soc.24.1.423.

Bunt, Gary R. *Hashtag Islam: How Cyber-Islamic Environments are Transforming Religious Authority*. Chapel Hill, NC: University of North Carolina Press, 2018.

Cherlin, Andrew J. "The Deinstitutionalization of American Marriage." *Journal of Marriage and Family* 66, no. 4 (2004): 848–61. http://dx.doi.org/10.1111/j.0022-2445.2004.00058.x.

Dunn, James D. G. *Unity and Diversity in the New Testament: An Inquiry into the Character of Earliest Christianity*. London: SCM Press, 1977.

Eller, Jack David. "Christianity Evolving: On the Origin of Christian Species." In *The End of Christianity*, edited by John W. Loftus, 23–51. Amherst, N.Y.: Prometheus Books, 2011.

———. *Introducing Anthropology of Religion: Culture to the Ultimate*. 2nd ed. New York: Routledge, 2015. https://doi.org/10.4324/9781315740157.

Freeze. Gregory L. "Subversive Atheism: Soviet Antireligious Campaigns and the Religious Revival in Ukraine in the 1920s." In *State Secularism and Lived Religion in Soviet Russia and Ukraine*. Edited by Catherine Wanner, 27–62. New York: Oxford University Press, 2012.

Grayzel, Solomon. *A History of the Jews: From the Babylonian Exile to the Present*. New York: The New American Library, 1968.

Hourani, Albert. *Arabic Thought in the Liberal Age, 1798–1939*. New York: Oxford University Press, 1962. https://doi.org/10.1017/cbo9780511801990.

Howard, Kenneth W. "The Religion Singularity: A Demographic Crisis Destabilizing and Transforming Institutional Christianity." *International Journal of Religion and Spirituality in Society* 7, no. 2 (2017): 77–93. http://dx.doi.org/10.18848/2154-8633/cgp/v07i02/77-93.

Lyotard, Jean-François. *The Postmodern Condition: A Report on Knowledge*. 1979. Translated by Geoff Bennington and Brian Massumi. Reprint, Minneapolis, MN: University of Minnesota Press, 1984.

Martin, David. "Pentecostalism: An Alternative Form of Modernity and Modernization?" In *Global Pentecostalism in the 21st Century*. Edited by Robert W. Hefner, 37–62. Bloomington, IN: Indiana University Press, 2013.

Orta, Andrew. "Converting Difference: Metaculture, Missionaries, and the Politics of Locality." *Ethnology* 37, no. 2 (Spring 1998): 165–85. http://dx.doi.org/10.2307/3774002.

Shorter, Aylward. *Toward a Theology of Inculturation.* Eugene, OR: Wipf & Stock, 2006.

Slade, Darren M. "Religious Homophily and Biblicism: A Theory of Conservative Church Fragmentation." *The International Journal of Religion and Spirituality in Society* 9, no. 1 (2019): 13–28. http://dx.doi.org/10.18848/2154-8633/cgp/v09i01/13-28.

Stark, Rodney, and Laurence R. Iannaccone. "A Supply-Side Reinterpretation of the 'Secularization' of Europe." *Journal for the Scientific Study of Religion* 33, no. 3 (September 1994): 230–52. https://doi.org/10.2307/1386688.

ABOUT THE AUTHOR

Jack David Eller holds a PhD in anthropology and has conducted fieldwork on religion and religious change among Australian Aboriginals. His other areas of interest include ethnic and religious violence, and he is the author of a number of books on cultural anthropology, anthropology of religion, psychological anthropology, and atheism/secularism.

MORE FROM THE AUTHOR

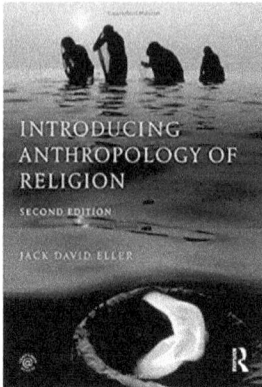

***Introducing Anthropology of Religion,
2nd ed.***
(2015, Routledge)

Jack David Eller

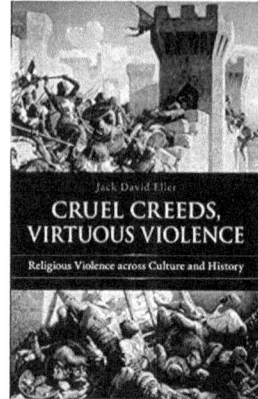

***Cruel Creeds, Virtuous Violence:
Religious Violence Across Culture
and History***
(2010, Prometheus)

Jack David Eller

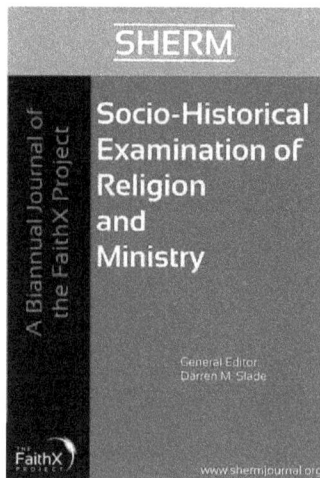

Piecing Together the "Book of the Chronicles of the Kings of Judah/Israel"

Lorence Yufa, Rubin Marshak, and Chris Shea-Kurek

The book of Kingdoms provides many hints to two of its sources, the "Book of the Chronicles of the Kings of Judah/Israel." Like many other scholars, we here at Milwaukee Atheists wonder what else this lost piece of history contains. Are all kings included? Who wrote this kings list and when? What gems are hidden in its pages? These may be questions too difficult to answer with current information. That's why Milwaukee Atheists is taking on plenty of other questions and topics related to religious history and biblical scholarship.

This organization formed in December 2014 and its members have studied diligently in fields of science, philosophy, history, and religion. With a weekly bible reading show that concentrates on getting to authorship and historical context of the text and a series of documentaries, we strive for authenticity and accuracy. Just like any other person interested in finding out what is true, our members and writers are always learning and follow the evidence where it leads. With in depth videos covering topics such as the Council of Nicaea, Marcion of Sinope, The Golden Calf, Mosaic authorship, and more, this YouTube channel has something for experts and laypeople.

Lorence Yufa is a lead writer of Milwaukee Atheists and the official video editor. He has spent the last decade debating creationists and other religious people on YouTube, Facebook, and other forums. For the past few years, he has been interested in biblical scholarship and religious history. He is currently attending UW-Milwaukee to earn a degree in religious studies.

Rubin Marshak is the writer of Armchair Philosophy. He holds a BA in Philosophy from the University of Wisconsin-Milwaukee. He also is a contributing member to Atheist Sunday School and creates all of the custom music and audio clips for our video content. He is now attending UWM for a degree in Psychology.

Chris Shea-Kurek is an information scientist, with a background in web design and development. He works on animations, art and design for the YouTube channel and the website. Chris also works on the set with green screening, studio set up, camera, sound and streaming.

Milwaukee Atheists:
Biblical Scholarship from a
Secular Perspective
Youtube.com/c/MilwaukeeAtheists

SHERM 1/1 (2019): 40–49

Conditions for the Great Religion Singularity

Brian D. McLaren,
The Convergence Network

Abstract: Applying the Buddhist "law of interdependent origination," which states that if the conditions are right, a particular phenomenon may exist, Brian McLaren provides ten conditional factors that he believes have contributed to Ken Howard's "religion singularity" (i.e. the multi-faceted collapse of institutional Christianity). Each condition falls under two main categories: either a lack of rapid adaptability in religious institutions or the moral failure of institutional leaders. The ten conditional factors include authoritarian centralization, betrayal of the religious founder's non-violence, a history of unacknowledged atrocities, military imperialism, white supremacy, scandals, reaction against scientific inquiry, doubling down on dualism, integrated and change-averse institutional systems, and paralysis and nostalgia.

Keywords: Religion Singularity, Interdependent Origination, Institutional Christianity, Adaptability, Moral Failure

Introduction

ONE OF BUDDHISM'S MANY gifts to the world is the principle of *pratityasamutpada*, which is sometimes named negatively as the "law of no independent origination" but is, perhaps, better translated positively as the "law of interdependent origination."[1] Like profound Christian mysteries such as the Trinity or *creatio continua*, or the transforming power of faith, this Buddhist teaching has many levels of meaning and has engendered all kinds of controversy. But one incontrovertible dimension of the teaching can be simply stated: if the conditions are right, something may exist. If the conditions are not right, it will not exist. In other words, the existence of anything is dependent on the conditions that produce it or on the conditions that it requires, and everything that exists is interdependent with its environment.[2]

Jesus articulated something similar in his parable of the soils (Mark 4:3–20). Even good seed will not grow unless the conditions are right, such as fertile soil, sufficient depth to retain moisture, absence of weeds that would compete for nutrients and sunlight, and so on. The parable goes beyond Paul's dictum that we reap what we sow, suggesting that even if we sow good seed, unsuitable external conditions can preclude a good harvest. The teachings of both Jesus and the Buddha invite us to step beyond our simple linear concepts of causality in order to think in deeper terms of sufficient conditions and, deeper still, in terms of webs or systems of interdependent conditions.

---

[1] For a brief summary of this principle, including why, in Buddhism, it is often linked to atheism, see Barbara O'Brien, "The Principle of Dependent Origination in Buddhism," ThoughtCo, April 5, 2018, https://www.thoughtco.com/dependent-origination-meaning-449723.

[2] Cf. Ewing Chinn, "Nāgārjuna's Fundamental Doctrine of *Pratītyasamutpāda*," *Philosophy East and West* 51, no. 1 (January 2001): 54–72, https://doi.org/10.1353/pew.2001.0005.

Socio-Historical Examination of Religion and Ministry
Volume 1, Issue 1, Spring 2019 www.shermjournal.org
© *Wipf and Stock Publishers. All Rights Reserved.*
Permissions: shermeditor@gmail.com
ISSN 2637-7519 (print), ISSN 2637-7500 (online)
https://doi.org/10.33929/sherm.2019.vol1.no1.05 (article)

WIPF *and*
STOCK
Publishers

The "religion singularity," as predicted by Ken Howard, is based on two observations, and each observation is interdependent with a number of interactive conditions that contributed to it. First, traditional religious engagement is declining in most parts of the West. Second, as engagement has been declining, the number of religious institutions has been rising. These two seemingly contradictory realities create the conditions for a new predicted reality: a religion singularity when religious institutions collapse or implode in large numbers.[3]

The first observation regarding the decline in religious engagement in the West has been widely researched and theories abound as to its causes. The second observation regarding the rising number of religious institutions has, to my knowledge, received less attention. Keeping the principle of interdependent origination in mind, I would suggest that a complex and dynamic set of conditions has led to these two observations, rendering the *Great Religion Singularity* (i.e. a multi-faceted collapse of institutional Christianity) not only possible, but virtually inevitable, barring the sudden rise of other radically disruptive conditions.[4]

These many specific and complexly interrelated conditions can be, I believe, organized under two general headings:

General Condition A (GCA): Institutional Brittleness; the lack of rapid adaptability in all major religious institutions, coupled with a rapidly changing environment, has led to a growing sense of cultural irrelevance and unfitness, resulting in declining religious retention in each generation, with cascading effects.

General Condition B (GCB): Moral Failure; the notable moral failures of religious leaders, members, and whole communities, leading to a fresh analysis of moral failures across history, which has made claims of one religion's spiritual supremacy over others literally incredible and ethically reprehensible.

Below, I will survey ten more specific examples of these general conditions.[5] I will also include "GCA" or "GCB" in parentheses to indicate which general condition is most linked to each example. Obviously, these specific examples could be explored to more and more granular levels of specificity. Here are some of the conditions that I see creating the backdrop for a *Great Religion Singularity* in the near future.

1. Authoritarian Centralization

Relatively early in its history, Christianity experienced a centrifugal force as charismatic leaders arose in response to political, economic, and other conditions. These *ad hoc* leaders formed various sects that decentralized the young faith. For example, in addition to a center in

---

[3] Kenneth W. Howard, "The Religion Singularity: A Demographic Crisis Destabilizing and Transforming Institutional Christianity," *International Journal of Religion and Spirituality in Society* 7, no. 2 (2017): 77–93, http://dx.doi.org/10.18848/2154-8633/cgp/v07i02/77-93.

[4] Such disruptive conditions might include nuclear, biological, or chemical warfare, an unforeseen planetary catastrophe, or something else entirely.

[5] I focus my attention here on Christianity (or Christianities) as the West's primary religious heritage, although conditions that affect Christianity often affect other traditions, as well.

Jerusalem associated with James, a new center emerged in Antioch, associated with Paul.[6] This multi-centeredness, flexibility, and adaptability are characteristic of a vibrant movement.

However, in response, institutional leaders struggled to consolidate power, regulate doctrine and liturgy, and maintain a sense of unity over Christianity's first few centuries. Unity was maintained by articulating essential doctrines, liturgical forms, and systems of authority (polity). Anyone who challenged these doctrines, liturgies, and polities was deemed a "heretic" (i.e. one who makes his own choices, as opposed to acquiescing to the choices made by institutional leaders). Heretics were subject to excommunication, imprisonment, torture, banishment, or death. This centralizing and authoritarian response was inherently conservative and made adaptation difficult, chiefly since adaptation equals change, and change equals heresy, and heresy carries the risk of great punishment.[7] (GCA)

2. Betrayal of Its Founder's Non-Violence

Sociologically, many streams of early Christianity adopted a non-Jewish identity and an anti-Semitic tone very early on.[8] The reasons for this turn are many and complex, as detailed by Kwame Bediako and others.[9] While some early Christians maintained a strong link with the Jewishness of their founder, others identified more with Greco-Roman culture, others with barbarian culture, and still others with a charismatic leader and his/her prejudices, etc. Together, they adopted various forms of supersessionism, claiming Christians had replaced the Jews as "God's chosen people."[10]

As a result, by the fourth century, Roman Christianity was decidedly anti-Semitic, and often violently so.[11] A long and tragic saga of anti-Semitic violence continued through the Reformation and culminated in the Holocaust, which the Christian faith has yet to fully acknowledge and repent of its complicity. Since being "postmodern" means to be post-Holocaust, this largely unacknowledged anti-Semitic history has undermined the credibility of Christianity, particularly over the last few generations.[12] (GCB)

3. History of Unacknowledged Atrocities

Institutional Christianity's early anti-Semitic turn represented a profound betrayal of the non-violent love-ethic of the religion's founder, Jesus Christ, which would pave the way for a

---

[6] See Ray S. Anderson, *An Emergent Theology for Emerging Churches* (Downers Grove, IL: InterVarsity Press, 2006), 12–15, 21–24, 51–52, 203–5. For diversity in the following generations of Christian leaders, see Kwame Bediako, *Theology and Identity: The Impact of Culture Upon Christian Thought in the Second Century and in Modern Africa*, Regnum Studies in Mission (1999; repr., Eugene, OR: Wipf and Stock Publishers, 2011).

[7] Harvey Cox, *The Future of Faith* (New York: HarperOne, 2009), 99–111. See also Vincent Donovan's analysis of current homogenizing and centralizing tendencies in Vincent J. Donovan, *The Church in the Midst of Creation* (Maryknoll, NY: Orbis Books, 1989).

[8] See Kenneth W. Howard, *Excommunicating the Faithful: Jewish Christianity in the Early Church*, 3rd ed. (Germantown, MD: FaithX Press, 2013).

[9] See Bediako, *Theology and Identity*, esp. 114–15.

[10] Cf. Seth Postell, "The Relevance of Jewish Identity for Ecclesiology," *Faith and Mission* 21, no. 3 (Summer 2004): 5–21.

[11] See James Carroll, *Constantine's Sword: The Church and the Jews, a History* (New York: Mariner Books, 2002).

[12] Cf. Michael E. Lodahl, "Christo-Praxis: Foundations for a Post-Holocaust Ethical Christology," *Journal of Ecumenical Studies* 30, no. 2 (Spring 1993): 213–25.

widening range of moral atrocities in the centuries to come, from sustained episodes of ethnic cleansing and genocide, to the longstanding suppression of women, to the church's complex and acrimonious relationship with LGBTQ persons. In the post-Holocaust era, as anti-Semitism became a source of shame, Western Christians seemed to lack a foil, and many shifted the focus of their animus from Jews to Muslims (in general) and Arabs (in particular). In an increasingly pluralistic world, this religious animus further undermines Christianity's credibility in the early twenty-first century.[13] (GCB)

4. Military Imperialism

Very early on, institutional Christianity further distanced itself from the non-violent ethic of its founder when its bishops submitted to Emperor Constantine. The cross, which had originally symbolized the extreme violence of Rome, had been inverted by these Christians to symbolize nonviolent love, forgiveness, and reconciliation between God and humanity. But with Constantine's conversion to Christianity, Jesus' subversion was itself subverted, and the cross once again became a symbol of imperial domination and all that it entailed. In this way, the bishops boosted the empire's power as a military and economic force, swelled the church's coffers, and raised the church's social status. In so doing, however, they drained the Christian faith of much of its moral authority and ethical distinctiveness.[14]

Of particular note, the same imperialistic urge to violently dominate "the other" has shown itself to be interdependent with an urge to violently dominate the earth, as well, leaving Christianity complicit in its contemporary ecological crises and impending climate catastrophe. The glaring failure of the church, so far at least, to challenge effectively the imperial economy's exploitation of the earth will likely become an increasingly significant reason for its marginalization in the years ahead.[15] (GCB)

5. White Supremacy

As institutional Christianity became more and more centered in Europe, it became increasingly racialized as a white religion. This racialization was powerfully intensified with the Doctrine of Discovery in the mid-fifteenth century. The Doctrine of Discovery authorized the white Christian kings of Europe to go into the world and make slaves of all non-Christian nations, confiscating their wealth, resources, and labor. It also created a series of European "Christian" empires, including, most notably, the Spanish and British Empires that covered vast

---

[13] I address some of these atrocities in Brian D. McLaren, *A New Kind of Christianity: Ten Questions That Are Transforming the Faith*, Pbk. ed. (New York: HarperCollins, 2011) and *The Great Spiritual Migration: How the World's Largest Religion Is Seeking a Better Way to Be Christian* (New York: Convergent Books, 2016). See also, Mae Elise Cannon et al., *Forgive Us: Confessions of a Compromised Faith* (Grand Rapids, MI: Zondervan, 2014) and Bruxy Cavey, *The End of Religion: Encountering the Subversive Spirituality of Jesus* (Colorado Springs, CO: NavPress, 2007), esp. 57–69.

[14] For more on Christian faith and militarism, see Brian Zahnd, *A Farewell to Mars: An Evangelical Pastor's Journey Toward the Biblical Gospel of Peace* (Colorado Springs, CO: David C. Cook, 2014) and *Postcards from Babylon: The Church in American Exile* (St. Joseph, MO: Spello Press, 2019).

[15] Cf. Mark I. Wallace, "The New Green Christianity: Why the Church Is Vital to Saving the Planet," *Word and World* 28, no. 1 (Winter 2008): 75–85.

parts of the globe until the 1970s.[16] In a long process, starting with the abolition movements of the eighteenth and nineteenth centuries, and then again in the Civil Rights movement of the 1960s, white supremacy has been exposed (even among many white people) as a crime against humanity. The continuing (often unconscious) embrace of white supremacy (evidenced in the infamous 80% of white evangelicals who supported Donald Trump's racist 2016 presidential campaign) has further eroded the moral standing of Western Christianity.[17] (GCB)

6. Scandals

With the rise of investigative journalism and the ubiquity of uncensored mass and social media, a series of religious scandals have been highly publicized in recent decades, from the financial and sexual misdeeds of Protestant televangelists in the 1990s to the pedophilia and cover-ups of Catholic and Southern Baptist hierarchy more recently.[18] No doubt, similar scandals occurred throughout Christian history, but reports were more easily suppressed when the church occupied a more influential position in society and when the media was more easily censored. Now, to see clergy shame people for abortion or LGBTQ identity, while they are covering up their own heinous actions, rightly disaffects millions from their churches and adds to the growing category of the SBNR ("spiritual but not religious") category. (GCB)

7. Reaction Against Scientific Inquiry

Meanwhile, the church has been in a reactionary mode in relation to science for over five centuries. The Roman Catholic Church's response to Copernicus and Galileo was echoed by most Protestants, and the dual doctrines of biblical inerrancy and papal infallibility were articulated during this period as a bulwark against scientific challenges to ecclesial dogma. While claims of infallibility or inerrancy may have strengthened the loyalty of insiders, they also created an exodus of people who found such claims intellectually dishonest. Increasingly, the universe described by many sectors of the church—6,000 years old, created by fiat in six literal days—became untenable for those who saw the Big Bang, an expanding universe, and biological evolution as being more honest and more likely than church dogma.[19] (GCA)

---

[16] For more on the Doctrine of Discovery, see McLaren, *The Great Spiritual Migration*, 71–123.

[17] Cf. Stephen Mansfield, *Choosing Donald Trump: God, Anger, Hope, and Why Christian Conservatives Supported Him* (Grand Rapids, MI: Baker Books, 2017); "No, That New Study Doesn't Debunk the Stat About 80 Percent of White Evangelicals Voting for Trump," Relevant, October 18, 2018, https://relevantmagazine.com/culture/politics-culture/no-that-new-study-doesnt-debunk-the-stat-about-80-percent-of-white-evangelicals-voting-for-trump/; and Kevin S. Seybold, "A Cultural Cognition Perspective on Religion Singularity: How Political Identity Influences Religious Affiliation," *Socio-Historical Examination of Religion and Ministry* 1, no. 1 (Spring 2019): 21–28, https://doi.org/10.33929/sherm.2019.vol1.no1.03.

[18] See for example, Laurie Goodstein and Sharon Otterman, "Catholic Priests Abused 1,000 Children in Pennsylvania, Report Says," *New York Times*, August 14, 2018, nytimes.com/2018/08/14/us/catholic-church-sex-abuse-pennsylvania.html; Elvia Malagon, "More Than 500 Priests Accused of Sexual Abuse Not yet Publicly Identified by Catholic Church, Illinois Attorney General Finds," *Chicago Tribune*, December 20, 2018, chicagotribune.com/news/local/breaking/ct-met-illinois-attorney-general-catholic-priest-abuse-20181219-story.html; and Robert Downen, Lise Olsen, and John Tedesco, "Abuse of Faith," *Houston Chronicle*, February 10, 2019, houstonchronicle.com/news/investigations/article/Southern-Baptist-sexual-abuse-spreads-as-leaders-13588038.php.

[19] Cf. Antony Alumkal, *Paranoid Science: The Christian Right's War on Reality* (New York: New York University Press, 2017), https://doi.org/10.2307/j.ctt1ggjjcz.

8. Doubling Down on Dualism

On a more philosophical level, institutional Christianity had very early on aligned itself with various forms of Neoplatonism. This philosophical commitment assumed that creation had two components: a spiritual component of ideal and immutable essences that included souls, moral laws, etc., a material component that included everything else.[20] This dualistic outlook presented the human being as a ghost in a machine, a spiritual essence inhabiting a material body. As scientific descriptions of the human being developed in recent centuries, through Darwin, Freud, and, more recently, neurobiology, this dualistic anthropological model has become unstable, unconvincing, and in many cases, untenable. Religious leaders have struggled to come to terms with the implications of these anthropological shifts in areas of sexuality, mental illness, psycho-pharmacology, and heuristics.[21] As a result, as is the case with the outer universe, the inner universe described by religious communities has felt increasingly distant from and irreconcilable with the universe understood and experienced by millions of people, driving them away from religious communities. While Christian scholars have grappled creatively and responsibly with these challenges, their work has been suppressed both intentionally and unconsciously, and the traditional language of liturgy and hymns has further reified the old dualistic framework. (GCA)

9. Integrated and Change-Averse Institutional Systems

The church, like any living organism, has evolved over time. It represents a complex aggregation of symbiotic systems. Sophisticated public relations, government relations, internal governance, economic, communication, education, service, property management, and investment systems (among others) brought many modern church institutions to their pinnacle of influence, wealth, and power in the early to mid-twentieth century. However, the systems of late-modern civilization have been changing with extreme speed, and many church systems have been unable to keep pace.

For example, a single technical advance, the tractor, led to profound changes in agriculture, with the small family farm giving way to huge agri-business enterprises. As a result, thousands of small towns have shrunk as farm labor was replaced by automation and millions migrated to urban centers to find new kinds of work. Today, denominations continue to send ministers to the buildings they erected in these once-thriving rural communities, even though the people have moved away. They have failed to anticipate these changes and devise pro-active responses that would both serve those who remain in rural areas and connect with the urbanizing majority. (GCA)

---

[20] See John Dillon, "Logos and Trinity: Patterns of Platonist Influence on Early Christianity," in *The Philosophy in Christianity*, ed. Godfrey Vesey, Royal Institute of Philosophy Lecture Series 25 (New York: Cambridge University Press, 1989), 1–13, https://doi.org/10.1017/s0957042x00011214; Thomas E. Gaston, "The Influence of Platonism on the Early Apologists," *Heythrop Journal: A Bimonthly Review of Philosophy and Theology* 50, no. 4 (July 2009): 573–80, https://doi.org/10.1111/j.1468-2265.2008.00448.x; and Roger E. Olson, *The Story of Christian Theology: Twenty Centuries of Tradition and Reform* (Downers Grove, IL: InterVarsity Press, 1999), 36, 54–67, 80, 85–98, 103–6, 174–93.

[21] Cf. Robert S. Weathers, "Dualism or Holism? A Look at Biblical Anthropology, Ethics, and Human Health," *Journal of the American Scientific Affiliation* 35, no. 2 (June 1983): 80–83.

10. Paralysis and Nostalgia

Because of the changes and challenges above, institutional leaders have been preoccupied with problem-solving in the aftermath of change and have not had sufficient energy or imagination to think and plan creatively about the opportunities of the present and the future. They bring assumptions about buildings, budgets, and measures of success that may be irrelevant and potentially counterproductive in the world today, not to mention the world five, ten, or fifty years from now. As leaders and congregants alike feel this stress, many have given up on adaptation and have chosen regression instead, nostalgically dreaming of a golden age. This nostalgia makes them form alliances with conservative or regressive political leaders who promise to bring them back to a set of conditions that were more hospitable to their familiar ways of thinking and living. (GCA)

Conclusion

I am among those who hoped that a renewal movement could arise across the many sectors of Christianity that would address these issues. Such a movement would practice a non-authoritarian and decentralized understanding of Christian faith. It would soberly and deeply acknowledge our betrayal of our Jewish founder's prime directive of non-violent, non-discriminatory love, and it would re-embrace revolutionary love as our *raison d'être*, including a love for the earth upon which we all depend. In particular, it would mobilize to help create a post-imperial, post-colonial, anti-racist, and post-supremacist world. It would work with a spirit of humility in light of its past public and personal failings and would enter into deep dialogue and collaboration with the scientific community, working for the common good. It would take decisive steps to re-allocate current institutional resources and foster a spirit of hope.

Although I still believe such a renewal movement is possible, I now lean toward the likelihood that some sort of collapse—or singularity—will occur, and something new will arise from institutional Christianity's ashes and rubble (at worst) or its confusion and paralysis (at best). If this expectation is accurate, what we anticipate is less a matter of renewal and more a matter of resurrection. Or to change the metaphor, we do not see ourselves in a temporary cold snap in the middle of a long summer. Instead, we are preparing for winter, knowing that spring will come, new leaves and blossoms will replace last year's fallen leaves, and the seeds we plant will grow once again.

Drawing from the principle of "no independent origination," we are less likely to see the future as predictable and certainly not as predetermined because we ourselves make choices that change the conditions in which the future will take shape. For that reason, we feel empowered, as protagonists with 7.2 billion other human beings in our shared story. Thus, we seek to align our efforts for the common good, knowing that "the common good" is always an ideal that we are seeking to understand more clearly, even as we seek it. This understanding, though hopeful in the long run, is neither a triumphalist nor complacent stance in the short run. In fact, this understanding is itself a condition that should engender a sense of sobriety, urgency, dedication, and care; or, in the words of the New Testament, a spirit of empowerment, love, and a sound mind (2 Tim. 1:7).

BIBLIOGRAPHY

Alumkal, Antony. *Paranoid Science: The Christian Right's War on Reality*. New York: New York University Press, 2017. https://doi.org/10.2307/j.ctt1ggjjcz.

Anderson, Ray S. *An Emergent Theology for Emerging Churches*. Downers Grove, IL: InterVarsity Press, 2006.

Bediako, Kwame. *Theology and Identity: The Impact of Culture Upon Christian Thought in the Second Century and in Modern Africa*. 1999. Regnum Studies in Mission. Reprint, Eugene, OR: Wipf and Stock Publishers, 2011.

Cannon, Mae Elise, Lisa Sharon Harper, Troy Jackson, and Soong-Chan Rah. *Forgive Us: Confessions of a Compromised Faith*. Grand Rapids, MI: Zondervan, 2014.

Carroll, James. *Constantine's Sword: The Church and the Jews, a History*. New York: Mariner Books, 2002.

Cavey, Bruxy. *The End of Religion: Encountering the Subversive Spirituality of Jesus*. Colorado Springs, CO: NavPress, 2007.

Chinn, Ewing. "Nāgārjuna's Fundamental Doctrine of *Pratītyasamutpāda*." *Philosophy East and West* 51, no. 1 (January 2001): 54–72. https://doi.org/10.1353/pew.2001.0005.

Cox, Harvey. *The Future of Faith*. New York: HarperOne, 2009.

Dillon, John. "Logos and Trinity: Patterns of Platonist Influence on Early Christianity." In *The Philosophy in Christianity*, edited by Godfrey Vesey. Royal Institute of Philosophy Lecture Series 25, 1–13. New York: Cambridge University Press, 1989. https://doi.org/10.1017/s0957042x00011214.

Donovan, Vincent J. *The Church in the Midst of Creation*. Maryknoll, NY: Orbis Books, 1989.

Gaston, Thomas E. "The Influence of Platonism on the Early Apologists." *Heythrop Journal: A Bimonthly Review of Philosophy and Theology* 50, no. 4 (July 2009): 573–80. https://doi.org/10.1111/j.1468-2265.2008.00448.x.

Howard, Kenneth W. *Excommunicating the Faithful: Jewish Christianity in the Early Church*. 3rd ed. Germantown, MD: FaithX Press, 2013.

———. "The Religion Singularity: A Demographic Crisis Destabilizing and Transforming Institutional Christianity." *International Journal of Religion and Spirituality in Society* 7, no. 2 (2017): 77–93. http://dx.doi.org/10.18848/2154-8633/cgp/v07i02/77-93.

Lodahl, Michael E. "Christo-Praxis: Foundations for a Post-Holocaust Ethical Christology." *Journal of Ecumenical Studies* 30, no. 2 (Spring 1993): 213–25.

Mansfield, Stephen. *Choosing Donald Trump: God, Anger, Hope, and Why Christian Conservatives Supported Him*. Grand Rapids, MI: Baker Books, 2017.

McLaren, Brian D. *The Great Spiritual Migration: How the World's Largest Religion Is Seeking a Better Way to Be Christian*. New York: Convergent Books, 2016

———. *A New Kind of Christianity: Ten Questions That Are Transforming the Faith*. Pbk. ed. New York: HarperCollins, 2011.

O'Brien, Barbara. "The Principle of Dependent Origination in Buddhism." ThoughtCo. April 5, 2018. https://www.thoughtco.com/dependent-origination-meaning-449723.

Olson, Roger E. *The Story of Christian Theology: Twenty Centuries of Tradition and Reform*. Downers Grove, IL: InterVarsity Press, 1999.

Postell, Seth. "The Relevance of Jewish Identity for Ecclesiology." *Faith and Mission* 21, no. 3 (Summer 2004): 5–21.

Relevant. "No, That New Study Doesn't Debunk the Stat About 80 Percent of White Evangelicals Voting for Trump." October 18, 2018. https://relevantmagazine.com/culture/politics-culture/no-that-new-study-doesnt-debunk-the-stat-about-80-percent-of-white-evangelicals-voting-for-trump/.

Seybold, Kevin S. "A Cultural Cognition Perspective on Religion Singularity: How Political Identity Influences Religious Affiliation." *Socio-Historical Examination of Religion and Ministry* 1, no. 1 (2019): 21–28, https://doi.org/10.33929/sherm.2019.vol1.no1.03.

Wallace, Mark I. "The New Green Christianity: Why the Church Is Vital to Saving the Planet." *Word and World* 28, no. 1 (Winter 2008): 75–85.

Weathers, Robert S. "Dualism or Holism? A Look at Biblical Anthropology, Ethics, and Human Health." *Journal of the American Scientific Affiliation* 35, no. 2 (June 1983): 80–83.

Zahnd, Brian. *A Farewell to Mars: An Evangelical Pastor's Journey Toward the Biblical Gospel of Peace.* Colorado Springs, CO: David C. Cook, 2014.

———. *Postcards from Babylon: The Church in American Exile.* St. Joseph, MO: Spello Press, 2019.

ABOUT THE AUTHOR

Brian D. McLaren is an author, speaker, activist, and public theologian. He is an Auburn Senior Fellow and a leader in the Convergence Network, through which he is developing an innovative training/mentoring program for pastors, church planters, and lay leaders called Convergence Leadership Project. McLaren works closely with the Center for Progressive Renewal, the Wild Goose Festival, and the Fair Food Program's Faith Working Group. His most recent joint project is an illustrated children's book (for all ages) called *Cory and the Seventh Story*.

MORE FROM THE AUTHOR

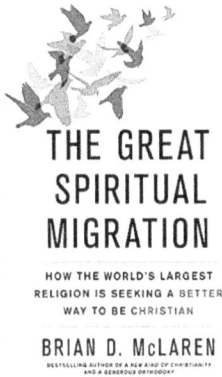

The Great Spiritual Migration: How the World's Largest Religion Is Seeking a Better Way to Be Christian
(2016, Convergent Books)

Brian D. McLaren

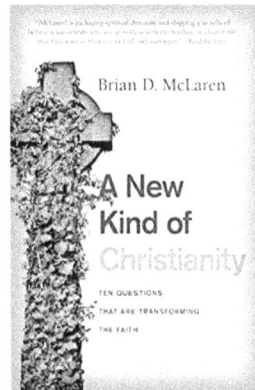

A New Kind of Christianity:
Ten Questions That Are Transforming the Faith (2010, HarperOne)

Brian D. McLaren

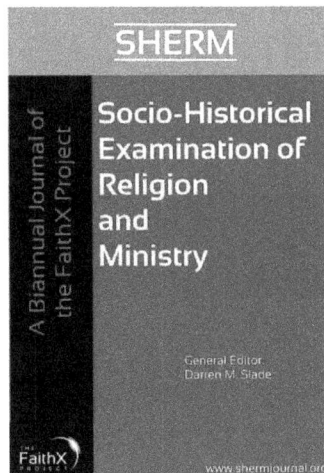

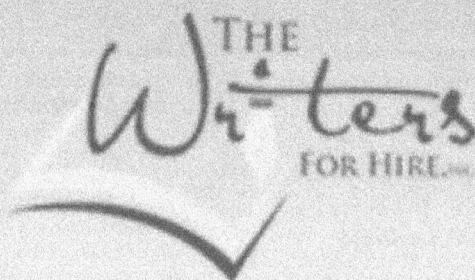

SHERM 1/1 (2019): 51–74

Responses to the Religion Singularity:
A Rejoinder

Darren M. Slade,
General Editor, SHERM Journal

Kenneth W. Howard,
Executive Direction, The FaithX Project

Editor's Note: This article and its research was sponsored by the FaithX Project.

Abstract: Since the publication of Kenneth Howard's 2017 article, "The Religion Singularity: A Demographic Crisis Destabilizing and Transforming Institutional Christianity," there has been an increasing demand to understand the root causes and historical foundations for why institutional Christianity is in a state of de-institutionalization. In response to Howard's research, a number of authors have sought to provide a contextual explanation for why the religion singularity is currently happening, including studies in epistemology, church history, psychology, anthropology, and church ministry. The purpose of this article is to offer a brief survey and response to these interactions with Howard's research, identifying the overall implications of each researcher's perspective for understanding the religion singularity phenomenon. It explores factors relating to denominational switching in Jeshua Branch's research, social memory in John Lingelbach's essay, religious politics in Kevin Seybold's survey, scientific reductionism in Jack David Eller's position paper, and institutional moral failure in Brian McLaren's article.

Keywords: Religion Singularity, Denominational Switching, Social Memory, Religious Politics, Scientific Reductionism, Christian Judgmentalism

Introduction

SINCE THE PUBLICATION OF Kenneth Howard's 2017 article, "The Religion Singularity: A Demographic Crisis Destabilizing and Transforming Institutional Christianity," there has been an increasing demand to understand the root causes and historical foundations for why institutional Christianity is, in a word, dying.[1] The trend toward non-institutional and fragmentary forms of religiosity is occurring not only in the West but across the globe, as well. What Howard's research indicates is that the percentage increase of new Christian denominations and worship centers is actually outpacing the plateaued percentage of Christian believers around the world. The inference being that churches and denominations are fragmenting (i.e. internally dividing due to conflict or other factors) faster than they are growing.[2] At its current rate of disintegration, institutional Christianity will have fragmented

---

[1] See for example, Darren M. Slade, "Religious Homophily and Biblicism: A Theory of Conservative Church Fragmentation," *The International Journal of Religion and Spirituality in Society* 9, no. 1 (2019): 13–28, http://dx.doi.org/10.18848/2154-8633/cgp/v09i01/13-28.

[2] Cf. C. Kirk Hadaway, "Is Evangelistic Activity Related to Church Growth?," in *Church and Denominational Growth*, ed. David A. Roozen and C. Kirk Hadaway (Nashville, TN: Abingdon, 1993), 169–87.

Socio-Historical Examination of Religion and Ministry
Volume 1, Issue 1, Spring 2019 www.shermjournal.org
© Wipf and Stock Publishers. All Rights Reserved.
Permissions: shermeditor@gmail.com
ISSN 2637-7519 (print), ISSN 2637-7500 (online)
https://doi.org/10.33929/sherm.2019.vol1.no1.06 (article)

WIPF *and*
STOCK
Publishers

itself into near extinction by the end of the twenty-first century, having been reduced to miniscule and, thus, financially unsustainable and culturally uninfluential congregational tribes (the "religion singularity").[3] In response to Howard's global and multi-denominational datasets, a number of researchers have sought to provide a contextual explanation for the religion singularity's emergence, including studies in epistemology, church history, psychology, anthropology, and church ministry. The purpose of this article is to offer a brief survey and response to these interactions with Howard's article, identifying the overall implications of each researcher's perspective for understanding the religion singularity phenomenon. It begins with a response to Jeshua Branch's epistemological approach to the subject matter.

Denominational Switching: A Response to Jeshua Branch

In Branch's article, "Grenz and Franke's Post-Foundationalism and the Religion Singularity," the author draws on the work of Stanley Grenz and John Franke (two prominent intellectuals who discuss Christianity's paradigm shift from modernity to postmodernity) to provide an epistemological context for the church's current destabilizing trend. Branch argues that the erosion of foundationalist principles that once sought absolute epistemological certainty has caused the emergence of post-foundationalism, which embraces diversity in theological beliefs. Dogmatic formulas and denominational allegiances no longer have the same social impact that they once did when Enlightenment attitudes permeated the church in the nineteenth and twentieth centuries. For Branch, it was strong foundationalism (as an arrogant epistemology) that incited internal conflict and division, forcing churches to break off into more and more competing congregations. However, as people became less enchanted with possessing or proclaiming absolute truth, the institutional nature of Christianity (in its various forms across the different sects) became less authoritative.[4] The result, according to Branch, is a trend toward nondenominational house churches that are less building-centric and less dependent on official ecclesial organization.[5]

Branch's article is an appropriate starting point for understanding the religion singularity by addressing the epistemological paradigms that may have aggravated denominational infighting, though we disagree with his presumption that institutional fragmentation may eventually subside in the future.[6] What is most interesting is his suggestion that post-foundationalist congregations attempt to curb theological division by openly embracing religious diversity (though, not necessarily religious pluralism). Of course, those who continue to advocate or practice Enlightenment-based foundationalism would likely argue that the paradigm shift into relative certainty (or wholesale uncertainty) is itself the root cause of Christianity's current problems.[7] Unfortunately, it is unlikely that post-foundationalism will

---

[3] Kenneth W. Howard, "The Religion Singularity: A Demographic Crisis Destabilizing and Transforming Institutional Christianity," *International Journal of Religion and Spirituality in Society* 7, no. 2 (2017): 77–93, http://dx.doi.org/10.18848/2154-8633/cgp/v07i02/77-93.

[4] Cf. Diana Butler Bass, *Christianity After Religion: The End of Church and the Birth of a New Spiritual Awakening* (New York: HarperCollins Publishers, 2012), esp. 11–99.

[5] Jeshua B. Branch, "Grenz and Franke's Post-Foundationalism and the Religion Singularity," *Socio-Historical Examination of Religion and Ministry* 1, no. 1 (Spring 2019): 1–9, https://doi.org/10.33929/sherm.2019.vol1.no1.01.

[6] Cf. Slade, "Religious Homophily and Biblicism," 18–23.

[7] See for example, Phil Johnson, "You Can't Handle the Truth: The Sinful Tolerance of Postmodernism," *The Journal of Modern Ministry* 1, no. 2 (Fall 2004): 219–45 and John F. MacArthur Jr., *The Truth War: Fighting for Certainty in an Age of Deception* (Nashville, TN: Thomas Nelson, 2007).

ever actually arrest church fragmentation, at least not in time to halt its de-institutionalization. Regardless, Branch's epistemological hypothesis makes sense as a dominant factor contributing to the religion singularity. Indeed, Howard devotes an entire chapter in his book, *Paradoxy*, to foundationalism, arguing it was Christianity's arrogant (foundationalist) belief that humans can eliminate subjectivity and accurately comprehend absolute truth that caused the church's current destabilization.[8]

While we agree with Branch's main thrust, we would argue that other elements of his essay appear to assume certain socio-historical beliefs about church ministry that are far too generalized. In his article, Branch briefly summarizes demographic data from selected surveys to demonstrate that so-called "conservative" churches have seen positive growth while so-called "liberal" (i.e. mainline) churches have declined. He suggests the two are related, which would seem to imply that Christians have been leaving mainline churches for conservative ones, though he is quick to clarify that both liberal and conservative churches are now in decline, resulting in a post-liberal and post-conservative trend in theology.[9] The problem is that it is difficult to extrapolate anything about this supposed liberal-conservative divide from these demographic surveys without a great deal of speculative assumptions. To begin, there is no question that in North America, from the 1960s until recently, mainline Protestant denominations have experienced at net numerical decline while conservative evangelical churches have experienced a steady net numerical increase.[10] However, it is not immediately apparent why this trend would be the case. According to one prominent theory, articulated here by Rodney Stark, "Americans mostly change churches in search of a deeper, more compelling faith," implying that stricter evangelical denominations are more spiritually vigorous than the ineffective traditions of mainline liberalism.[11] Not surprisingly, theorists have argued that conservative theologies are intricately linked to stricter ("high tension") churches, oftentimes being the underlying cause for other growth-related factors, including a congregation's sense of absolutism and missionary zeal. Accordingly, committed religionists tend to desire conservative theologies because, among other things, it promotes stricter adherence to the religion and provides a more satisfying, convictional, and self-assured message that abounds in feelings of epistemic security.[12]

There appears to be support for this speculation. A small group of researchers in Canada found that theological conservatism, oftentimes associated with greater moral strictness, was a

---

[8] Ken Howard, *Paradoxy: Creating Christian Community Beyond Us and Them* (Brewster, MA: Paraclete Press, 2010), 30–46.

[9] Branch, "Grenz and Franke's Post-Foundationalism," 5–7.

[10] For brief reviews of this trend in both Canada and the United States, see Kurt Bowen, *Christians in a Secular World: The Canadian Experience* (Montreal, Quebec: McGill-Queen's University Press, 2004), 276–79; Kevin N. Flatt, *After Evangelicalism: The Sixties and the United Church of Canada* (Montreal, Quebec: McGill-Queen's University Press, 2013), 229–49; Rodney Stark, *What Americans Really Believe: New Findings from the Baylor Surveys of Religion* (Waco, TX: Baylor University Press, 2008), 21–22; and Gregory Smith, *America's Changing Religious Landscape: Christians Decline Sharply as Share of Population; Unaffiliated and Other Faiths Continue to Grow* (Washington, DC: Pew Research Center, May 12, 2015), 4, 8, accessed April 3, 2019, https://www.pewforum.org/2015/05/12/americas-changing-religious-landscape/.

[11] See Stark, *What Americans Really Believe*, 21–25, 29–36; quote appears on p. 21.

[12] For these correlations, see Rodney Stark and Roger Finke, *Acts of Faith: Explaining the Human Side of Religion* (Berkeley, CA: University of California Press, 2000), 141–68 and Jeremy N. Thomas and Daniel V. A. Olson, "Testing the Strictness Thesis and Competing Theories of Congregational Growth," *Journal for the Scientific Study of Religion* 49, no. 4 (December 2010): 619–39, https://doi.org/10.1111/j.1468-5906.2010.01534.x.

significant element in predicting church growth, whereas theological liberalism was associated with churches in decline.[13] Roger Finke and Rodney Stark discovered the same thing when they found that even theologically conservative churches associated with mainline denominations grew while their liberal counterparts from the same denomination weakened.[14] In relation to Branch's epistemological survey, one study showed that congregants were attracted to certain churches specifically because the pastors expressed certainty about the absolute truthfulness of their preaching message.[15]

The liberal-conservative misconception

Regrettably, these types of studies often engage in a causal oversimplification when they attempt to divide denominations into "liberal-versus-conservative" congregations, reducing everything to mere theology. Yet, national polling data suggests that theology is not as important as some theorists would like to believe. For example, of the 49% of American adults who actively looked for a new church in the last few years, the majority (34%) said they did so simply because they had moved. Among evangelicals and mainline Protestants, almost half (49% and 45% respectively) said they looked for a new church for the same reason. Interestingly, 11% said they looked for a new church because they disagreed with the clergy, 7% cited other problems with their old church, and 5% claimed they had a change in their beliefs. Only 3% cited problems with their old church's theology as the reason for looking elsewhere. Likewise, 3% said they were exploring new beliefs, 1% stated their beliefs had evolved, and 1% cited an actual change in their religion or denomination. There was no statistically significant mention of anything to do with theology, doctrines, or beliefs. In fact, of the 71% who said finding a new church was easy, only 5% said it was easy because they agreed with the church's theology, the rest cited elements relating to convenience and a sense of community as the reason why they chose their new church. Correspondingly, of the 49% of Americans who searched for a different church, only 7% cited their disagreement with theology as the reason why it was difficult to find a new congregation. The majority of those who found it difficult again cited problems relating to convenience and a sense of community, not theology.[16] In other words, the reasons why people leave their church or join a new one almost never have anything to do with theology or doctrine. They have to do with more practical concerns of a social nature.

There is no clearer indication that theology has little to do with church growth than the actual principles, practices, and priorities of Christians themselves. As George Barna remarked

---

[13] It is important to note that the researchers compared churches within the same mainline Protestant denominations in the same geographical area (southern Ontario). Some of the congregations exhibited more conservative beliefs while other churches exhibited more liberal beliefs, though they were part of the same mainline denomination. See David Millard Haskell, Kevin N. Flatt, and Stephanie Burgoyne, "Theology Matters: Comparing the Traits of Growing and Declining Mainline Protestant Church Attendees and Clergy," *Review of Religious Research* 58, no. 4 (2016): 515–41, http://dx.doi.org/10.1007/s13644-016-0255-4.

[14] Roger Finke and Rodney Stark, *The Churching of America, 1776–2005: Winners and Losers in Our Religious Economy* (New Brunswick, NJ: Rutgers University Press, 2005), 276–79.

[15] Joseph B. Tamney and Stephen D. Johnson, "The Popularity of Strict Churches," *Review of Religious Research* 39, no. 3 (March 1998): 209–23, https://doi.org/10.2307/3512589.

[16] Alan Cooperman, *Choosing a New Church or House of Worship: Americans Look for Good Sermons, Warm Welcome* (Washington, DC: Pew Research Center, Aug. 23, 2016), 5, 11–13, 21–23, accessed April 3, 2019, https://www.pewforum.org/2016/08/23/choosing-a-new-church-or-house-of-worship/. Of the 49% who searched for a new church, 28% said it was difficult, of which 26% said it was difficult due to concerns over theology. Hence, only 7.29% of the original 49% cited anything to do with theology.

back in 2001, "Three of every five adult Christians we surveyed told us they want to have a deep commitment to the Christian faith, but they are not involved in any intentional effort to grow spiritually."[17] This lack of intentionality for a richer faith or greater spiritual commitment conflicts with the idea that Christians deliberately change churches for the purpose of joining a more theologically conservative denomination. Similarly, yearning for a stricter spiritual life appears inconsistent with the low number of Christians who actually take measurable steps to increase their spiritual development. At the turn of the century, only 24% of Christians participated in some form of Sunday school, 15% had a spiritual mentor, 11% attended classes designed to enhance spiritual maturity, and 30% of Christians confessed to having no plan or process in place to achieve any spiritual goals. Ultimately, less than 18% of Christians stated that growing spiritually was their biggest ambition in life.[18] Meanwhile, Diana Butler-Bass argues against the blanket assumption that conservative churches invariable grow while liberal churches invariably decline. From qualitative research, she has demonstrated that liberal churches with a clear sense of purpose actually tend to grow.[19] If theology or a deeper faith were truly the cause for liberal decline, surely more Christians would prioritize these very objectives in their own spiritual lives.

Moreover, the idea that evangelicalism grows because there is a mass exodus of disillusioned liberals is simply an over exaggeration of the actual data. According to Mark Chavez, the surge of liberal Protestants switching to conservative churches started to decelerate precisely when conservative churches began to grow. Barely 10% of mainline Christians born after 1970 switch to conservatism.[20] As indicated from a 2007 poll, the majority of those raised conservative merely switch to another conservative tradition. Liberal Christians, on the other hand, were more evenly split where approximately the same number of those raised in a mainline tradition retained their liberal affiliation as those who switched to a conservative tradition. In fact, the relocation rates between liberal and conservative denominations were almost identical where 31% of evangelicals had converted from a non-conservative denomination and 30% of mainline Christians had converted from a non-liberal tradition.[21] Currently, only 14% of those now professing to be evangelical say they were once raised liberal whereas 20% of current liberals say they were once raised conservative, indicating a potential shift in how American Christians associate with evangelicalism.[22] The data from these national polls depict a different understanding of denominational switching than the presumed belief about conservative dominance: liberal Christians are not deconverting to evangelical churches any more than conservative Christians are converting to mainline denominations. Attempts to switch

---

[17] George Barna, *Growing True Disciples: New Strategies for Producing Genuine Followers of Christ* (Colorado Springs, CO: WaterBrook Press, 2001), 34–35.

[18] Barna, *Growing True Disciples*, 35–42.

[19] Diana Butler Bass, *The Practicing Congregation: Imagining a New Old Church* (Herndon, VA: Alban Institute, 2004), 3–6.

[20] Mark Chaves, *American Religion: Contemporary Trends* (Princeton, NJ: Princeton University Press, 2011), 87–88, https://doi.org/10.23943/princeton/9780691146850.001.0001.

[21] Luis Lugo, *U.S. Religious Landscape Survey: Religious Affiliation; Diverse and Dynamic* (Washington, DC: Pew Research Center, Feb. 2008) 28, 31–32, accessed April 3, 2019, https://www.pewforum.org/2008/02/01/u-s-religious-landscape-survey-religious-affiliation/.

[22] See the demographics in Smith, *America's Changing Religious Landscape* 33–44.

denominations on either side are infrequent and are equally divided between those who switch traditions and those who retain the same denominational affiliation.

The point is that theology really has little to do with church growth and decline. Thus, when taking data samples from the top mainline denominations in the United States, one survey found that a congregation's beliefs did not substantially influence their numerical growth when other growth-related factors were considered, such as being externally focused (e.g. proselyting outsiders and engaging in social action), having superior programming, and providing a climate that fosters personal self-reflection. Because these factors are equally possible in both conservative and liberal assemblies, both types of churches are just as likely to grow numerically regardless of their doctrinal stances.[23] Hence, many theologically conservative churches decline as they experience the same reduction in membership and attendance rates as mainline denominations.[24] At the same time, some liberal churches continue to thrive congregationally, which indicates that there are other factors influencing growth rates apart from a mere conservative-liberal divide.[25]

The truth is that the decline of liberal mainline Protestantism was an historical phenomenon much like it was for liberalism's incredible growth during the second half of the nineteenth century.[26] Its historical demise is most likely the result of a religious reaction against progressive societal changes, coupled with the fact that conservatives have had higher birth rates and membership retention than their liberal counterparts.[27] The point is that correlation does not equate to causation, and oversimplified explanations rarely enjoy universal application. There is simply no real evidence to suggest that conservative beliefs actually cause numerical growth or congregational vitality. The situation is simply far more complex and is, therefore, not a useful paradigm with which to understand the causal factors surrounding the religion singularity.

---

[23] Cf. Daniel V. A. Olson, "Congregational Growth and Decline in Indiana Among Five Mainline Denominations," in *Church and Denominational Growth*, ed. David A. Roozen and C. Kirk Hadaway (Nashville, TN: Abingdon Press, 1993), 208–24 and Michael J. Donahue and Peter L. Benson, "Belief Style, Congregational Climate, and Program Quality," in *Church and Denominational Growth*, ed. David A. Roozen and C. Kirk Hadaway (Nashville, TN: Abingdon Press, 1993), 225–40.

[24] C. Kirk Hadaway and Penny Long Marler, "Growth and Decline in the Mainline," in *Faith in America: Changes, Challenges, New Directions*, ed. Charles H. Lippy, vol. 1, *Organized Religion Today* (Westport, CT: Praeger, 2006), 1–24; Chaves, *American Religion*, 92, 131n9; Howard, "The Religion Singularity," 78, 89.

[25] See Kevin D. Dougherty, Brandon C. Martinez, and Gerardo Martí "Congregational Diversity and Attendance in a Mainline Protestant Denomination," *Journal for the Scientific Study of Religion* 54, no. 4 (December 2015): 668–83, https://doi.org/10.1111/jssr.12229 and Jennifer March, "Reconsidering Mainline Decline: Contemporary Forms of Mainline Adaptation and Congregational Survival" (paper presented at the annual meeting of the American Sociological Association, Montreal, Quebec, 2006), 1–20.

[26] Sydney E. Ahlstrom, *A Religious History of the American People* (New Have, CT: Yale University Press, 1972), 763–84 and Hadaway and Marler, "Growth and Decline in the Mainline," 1–24.

[27] Cf. Penny Long Marler and C. Kirk Hadaway, "New Church Development and Denominational Growth (1950–1988): Symptom or Cause?," in *Church and Denominational Growth*, ed. David A. Roozen and C. Kirk Hadaway (Nashville, TN: Abingdon Press, 1993), 47–86; Bruce A. Greer, "Strategies for Evangelism and Growth in Three Denominations (1965–1990)," in *Church and Denominational Growth*, ed. David A. Roozen and C. Kirk Hadaway (Nashville, TN: Abingdon Press, 1993), 87–111; and Norman M. Green and Paul W. Light, "Growth and Decline in an Inclusive Denomination: The ABC Experience," in *Church and Denominational Growth*, ed. David A. Roozen and C. Kirk Hadaway (Nashville, TN: Abingdon Press, 1993), 112–26.

Social Memory: A Response to John Lingelbach

Next, we consider John Lingelbach's essay, "First Century Christian Diversity: Historical Evidence of a Social Phenomenon."[28] Here, Lingelbach compares the religion singularity to the diversity of the primitive church, focusing particularly on the years 30 to 100 CE. In this article, he conceives of the earliest form of Christian religion (the "pre-Pauline oral tradition") as having been thoroughly Jewish. Without explicitly stating it, the historical assumption appears to be that Jesus (a Second Temple Jew) passed along teachings directly to his apostles (also Jews), which were then disseminated across Palestine in oral form. By the middle of the first century, however, this primitive Christian movement broke into two dominant and influential sects, the Pauline church and the Ebionite church (the former predating the latter).[29] Subsequently, Lingelbach argues that not only did Pauline Christianity break from the apostles' original Jewish teachings (centered in Jerusalem) but that Ebionite Christianity broke away (in part) because of Paul's seeming rejection of Judaism.[30]

Howard, on the other hand, argues in *Paradoxy* that Paul viewed the original Jesus tradition as an a-religious movement, meaning it was indifferent and possibly even critical of "religion" to the point that Paul did not believe people needed to change their religion to follow Christ.[31] Nonetheless, Lingelbach concludes that "original" Christianity, which was initially persecuted by Paul, had quickly splintered into two main factions (one Jewish, the other Gentile) by the end of the first century.[32] The relationship of his article to the religion singularity is its

---

[28] John F. Lingelbach, "First Century Christian Diversity: Historical Evidence of a Social Phenomenon," *Socio-Historical Examination of Religion and Ministry* 1, no. 1 (Spring 2019): 11–20, https://doi.org/10.33929/sherm.2019.vol1.no1.02.

[29] The implication is most noticeable in Lingelbach's treatment of the "Nazarenes" as distinct from the Judaizing Ebionites (Lingelbach, "First Century Christian Diversity," 14, 17–18), as well as his suggestion that the Nazarenes may have predated the Apostle Paul's conversion, despite Epiphanius of Salamis (ca. 315–403) claiming that the Nazarene "heresy" first developed in the Decapolis toward the end of the first century (*Pan.* 29.7.7–8). This is also Howard's contention when he argues elsewhere that the Nazarene sect was likely the earliest expression of Christianity and, surprisingly, the longest lasting since it may have existed as late as the sixth century (Kenneth W. Howard, *Excommunicating the Faithful: Jewish Christianity in the Early Church*, 3rd ed. [Germantown, MD: FaithX Press, 2013], 22–27, 33–35). For more details on the Nazarene sect, see Martinus C. de Boer, "The Nazoreans: Living at the Boundary of Judaism and Christianity," in *Tolerance and Intolerance in Early Judaism and Christianity*, ed. Graham N. Stanton and Guy G. Stroumsa (New York: Cambridge University Press, 1998), 239–62, http://dx.doi.org/10.1017/cbo9780511659645.015; Craig R. Koester, "The Origin and Significance of the Flight to Pella Tradition," *The Catholic Biblical Quarterly* 51, no. 1 (January 1989): 90–106; P. H. R. van Houwelingen, "Fleeing Forward: The Departure of Christians from Jerusalem to Pella," *The Westminster Theological Journal* 65, no. 2 (Fall 2003): 181–200; and Daniel Boyarin, *Border Lines: The Partition of Judaeo-Christianity* (Philadelphia, PA: University of Pennsylvania Press, 2004), 1–33, https://doi.org/10.9783/9780812203844.

[30] This is an interesting suggestion considering that many scholars date the Ebionite movement to the second century as an offshoot of the Nazorean movement (see S. C. Mimouni, "Les nazoréens: Recherche étymologique et historique," *Revue Biblique* 105, no. 2 [1998]: 208–62). However, Lingelbach's theory does have affinities to Andries van Aarde's research on cultural identity in Ebionism (Andries G. van Aarde, "Ebionite Tendencies in the Jesus Tradition: The Infancy Gospel of Thomas Interpreted from the Perspective of Ethnic Identity," *Neotestamentica* 40, no. 2 [2006]: 353–82). Cf. Joan E. Taylor, "The Phenomenon of Early Jewish-Christianity: Reality or Scholarly Invention?," *Vigiliae Christianae* 44, no. 4 (1990): 313–34, http://dx.doi.org/10.1163/157007290x00090.

[31] Howard, *Paradoxy*, 47–65.

[32] Lingelbach, "First Century Christian Diversity," 15–19.

reiteration of Howard's assertion that theological diversity has been part of Christian tradition since its earliest days.[33]

Unfortunately, Lingelbach does not trace Christian diversity far back enough, hinting that the Christian church was quite homogenous (at least in fundamental beliefs, such as Christ's divinity) prior to splintering into Pauline and Ebionite forms. As such, Lingelbach appears to take the traditionally catholic and canonical viewpoint that there existed a type of "mother-church," led by the apostolic Twelve, whose base of operation was in Jerusalem (cf. Acts 2:41–42). From this geographic center came the apostolic faith of Christianity *par excellence*, though variations and elaborations eventually appeared over time. The implication is that there was an "original" or "pure" form of Christianity prior to these evolutionary and theological developments (Cf. Clement, *1 Clem.* 42.1–4; Tertullian, *Marc.* 4.7).[34] The problem is that this historical reconstruction, however nuanced, does not account for the nature of ancient oral traditions and their dissemination through social and collective memory.

Advances in the social sciences have demonstrated, particularly in the fields of historical Jesus research, that there likely never was an "original" form of Christianity, even from the apostles themselves. This conclusion becomes especially evident when considering the itinerant and contextual nature of Jesus' ministry and the subsequent multiplicity of interpretations about Jesus' person and message (even while Jesus was still alive; cf. Mark 8:27–29 and par.). The Christologies that existed prior to Jesus' crucifixion undoubtedly persisted afterwards, evidenced most pointedly by the fact that every instance of verbal communication is both unique and transitory to the specific biosphere of Jesus' nomadic oral performances.[35] As Elaine Pagels remarks, "We can see how both gnostic and orthodox forms of Christianity could emerge as variant interpretations of the teaching and significance of Christ."[36] Even Paul acknowledged multiple christological interpretations that conflicted with his own (cf. Gal 1.6–7; 2 Cor. 11:4; cf. 1 John 4:1). The point is that equiprimordiality, not singular originality, better characterizes the earliest pre-Pauline Jesus movement, meaning that oral cultures did not lend themselves to a single, "original" tradition like it would have in a print-dominant culture.[37] It is unlikely that there was a fixed or stable Jesus tradition prior to the written Gospels despite the apologetic determination of people like Birger Gerhardsson or Kenneth Bailey.[38]

This multiformity indicates that there existed many pre-Pauline Christiani*ties* and that neither Pauline nor Ebionite tradition popularized Christian diversity in the primitive church,

---

[33] Howard, "The Religion Singularity," 87, 90. See also, James M. Robinson and Helmut Koester, *Trajectories through Early Christianity* (1971; repr., Eugene, OR: Wipf and Stock Publishers, 2006).

[34] Lingelbach remarks, "Paul probably received an introduction to this initial version of Christianity from Peter and James three years after his conversion" (Lingelbach, "First Century Christian Diversity," 13). He later concludes, "The initial movement of Christianity was the movement persecuted by Paul" (p. 19).

[35] Alan Kirk, "Manuscript Tradition as A *Tertium Quid:* Orality and Memory in Scribal Practices," in *Memory and the Jesus Tradition: The Reception of Jesus in the First Three Centuries* (New York: Bloomsbury T&T Clark, 2018), 114–37, http://dx.doi.org/10.5040/9780567663474.0014; Walter J. Ong, *Orality and Literacy*, 3rd ed. (London: Routledge, 2012), 115–33, http://dx.doi.org/10.4324/9780203103258; Ruth H. Finnegan, *Literacy and Orality: Studies in the Technology of Communication* (Oxford, England: Basil Blackwell, 1988), 69.

[36] Elaine Pagels, *The Gnostic Gospels*, Pbk. ed. (1979; repr., New York: Vintage Books, 1989), 148.

[37] See esp., Werner H. Kelber, "In the Beginning Were the Words: The Apotheosis and Narrative Displacement of the Logos," in *Imprints, Voiceprints, and Footprints of Memory: Collected Essays of Werner h. Kelber*, Resources for Biblical Study (Atlanta, GA: SBL Press, 2013), 77–80, http://dx.doi.org/10.2307/j.ctt5hjh34.10 and Rafael Rodríguez, *Oral Tradition and the New Testament: A Guide for the Perplexed* (New York: Bloomsbury T&T Clark, 2014), https://doi.org/10.5040/9781472550675.

[38] See Eric Eve, *Behind the Gospels: Understanding the Oral Tradition* (2013; repr., Minneapolis, MN: Fortress Press, 2014), 33–46, 66–85.

though Lingelbach is correct to emphasize that these two movements were likely the most influential of the earliest breakaway movements. Considering that both the oral traditions and the variant written Gospels were meant for audial performances, variations and discrepancies in these stories would have been considered an appropriate use of artistic license.[39] In fact, ancient scribal practices reveal that texts were copied *from* oral performances *for* oral performances, which meant that changes to the Jesus tradition would have been expected and accepted in an oral-dominant culture.[40] Consequently, the nature of social memory in oral cultures actually heightens the premise that diversity was both inherent to and prolific in the primitive first century church long before Paul's Gentile breakaway.[41]

In terms of social and collective memory, the pre-Pauline and pre-textual traditions were largely a social phenomenon where the mere act of remembering was derived from and dependent upon pre-existing cultural structures. The implication is, once again, a reminder that *all* approaches to Christian faith, especially in the first century, are *interpretations* of people's localized and socially-constructed memory of personal experiences.[42] Most interesting for historical research is the suggestion that the Jesus traditions may have undergone rapid change immediately after Jesus' death as his followers interpreted their collective memories according to their post-Easter needs, which only then stabilized into a more fixed tradition later in the first century.[43] The point is that Lingelbach approaches church history from the standpoint of a *textual* perspective rather than from the more appropriate *oral* mindset of the primitive church, which would add even greater depth to his understanding of first-century Christian diversity.

Finally, Lingelbach concludes that the cosmopolitan sub-continent of Asia Minor may have served as a geographic nucleus for diverse belief systems, which is both captivating and historically plausible. Regrettably, this proposal is only briefly mentioned in Lingelbach's article and supported simply from the fact that different Christianities took root alongside each other in Asia Minor. Nonetheless, the idea that this region may have strengthened diversity, as seen in modern-day metropolises, is an exciting approach to studying the religion singularity. Further sociological research ought to be done on whether the cosmopolitan nature of Asia Minor would

---

[39] Cf. John Miles Foley, "Memory in Oral Tradition," in *Performing the Gospel: Orality, Memory, and Mark; Essays Dedicated to Werner Kelber*, Pbk. ed., ed. Richard A. Horsley, Jonathan A. Draper, and John Miles Foley (Minneapolis, MN: Fortress Press, 2011), 83–96; Albert B. Lord, *The Singer of Tales*, 2nd ed., ed. Stephen Mitchell and Gregory Nagy (Cambridge, MA: Harvard University Press, 2000), 99–125, 133; and Finnegan, *Literacy and Orality*, 69.

[40] A. N. Doane, "The Ethnography of Scribal Writing and Anglo-Saxon Poetry: Scribe as Performer," *Oral Tradition* 9, no. 2 (October 1994): 420–39; Raymond F. Person Jr., "The Ancient Israelite Scribe as Performer," *Journal of Biblical Literature* 117, no. 4 (Winter 1998): 601–9, http://dx.doi.org/10.2307/3266629; Katherine O'Brien O'Keeffe, *Visible Song: Transitional Literacy in Old English Verse* (New York: Cambridge University Press, 1990).

[41] Kirk, "Manuscript Tradition as A *Tertium Quid*," 114–37.

[42] See Maurice Halbwachs, *On Collective Memory*, ed. and trans. Lewis A. Coser (Chicago, IL: University of Chicago Press, 1992); Sandra Huebenthal, "Social and Cultural Memory in Biblical Exegesis: The Quest for an Adequate Application," in *Cultural Memory in Biblical Exegesis*, ed. Pernille Carstens, Trine Hasselbalch, and Niels Peter Lemche, Perspectives on Hebrew Scriptures and Its Contexts 17 (Piscataway, NJ: Gorgias Press, 2012), 175–99; and Alan Kirk, "Social and Cultural Memory," in *Memory, Tradition, and Text: Use of the Past in Early Christianity*, ed. Alan Kirk and Tom Thatcher, Semeia Studies 52 (Boston, MA: SBL, 2005), 1–24.

[43] See Darren M. Slade, "Miracle Eyewitness Reports," in *Encyclopedia of Psychology and Religion*, ed. David A. Leeming (Berlin, Heidelberg: Springer, 2018), http://dx.doi.org/10.1007/978-3-642-27771-9_200227-1 and the research in Eve, *Behind the Gospels*, 66–85.

have intensified Christian diversity (or if diversity was already at a sufficiently high level before reaching Asia Minor) just like, according to Lingelbach, the internet has done today.[44]

Religious Politics: A Response to Kevin Seybold

Kevin Seybold's position paper, "A Cultural Cognition Perspective on Religion Singularity: How Political Identity Influences Religious Affiliation," challenges conventional wisdom surrounding the relationship between religion and politics. As demographic surveys consistently show, many Christians, most notably white evangelicals, unquestioningly identify with the Republican Party. In fact, one 2008 study found that white evangelicals are more likely to claim Republican politicians are not conservative *enough* for their liking.[45] Demographics demonstrate that evangelicalism is now an ethnically regionalized culture-religion confined almost exclusively to lower income small towns in America's Southern and Midwest areas. As a narrow subculture within white America, these evangelicals have little in common with younger generations who are typically more diverse, more tolerant of alternative lifestyles, live in urban population centers, are politically moderate or liberal, college educated, and non-married.[46] What this potentially means for the study of religion and politics is that white evangelicalism might lessen in terms of being a reliable voting bloc, though their political influence remains steadfast for now.[47] Until then, the Republican Party can effectively rely on the white evangelical vote by employing alarmist rhetoric on a handful of emotionally-charged issues, which intend to galvanize, polarize, and distract religious voters.[48]

With this in mind, it has generally been assumed that most evangelicals vote Republican because they are Christian, but Seybold's article challenges this widely held assumption. Instead, he forces psychologists and sociologists to ask the opposite question: What if these voters identify as Republican first and, *because* of their political affiliation, subsequently consider themselves Christian? Utilizing cultural cognition theory, Seybold uses both psychological and sociological studies to expose the role of group identity in judgment formation. His conclusion is stimulating: the extreme polarization in American politics today

---

[44] Cf. Paul Trebilco, "Christian Communities in Western Asia Minor into the Early Second Century: Ignatius and Others as Witnesses Against Bauer," *Journal of the Evangelical Theological Society* 49, no. 1 (March 2006): 17–44 and Mikael Tellbe, "De Efesoskristna : Teologisk mångfald och social identitet i den tidiga kristna rörelsen," *Svensk Teologisk Kvartalskrift* 86, no. 1 (2010): 4–12.

[45] Andrew Kohut et al., *Some Social Conservative Disillusionment: More Americans Question Religion's Role in Politics* (Results from the 2008 Annual Religion and Public Life Survey) (Washington, DC: Pew Research Center, August 21, 2008), 16–18, accessed April 6, 2019, http://assets.pewresearch.org/wp-content/uploads/sites/5/legacy-pdf/445.pdf.

[46] Glenn H. Utter and John W. Storey, *The Religious Right: A Reference Handbook*, 3rd ed. (Millerton, NY: Grey House Publishing, 2007), 145–56; Smith, *America's Changing Religious Landscape*, 49–50, 68–77. See also the summary in Ronald J. Sider, *The Scandal of the Evangelical Conscience: Why Are Christians Living Just Like the Rest of the World?* (Grand Rapids, MI: Baker Books, 2005), 27–28.

[47] Cf. Robert P. Jones, *The End of White Christian America* (New York: Simon and Schuster Paperbacks, 2016), 110.

[48] See for example, Jason C. Bivins, *Religion of Fear: The Politics of Horror in Conservative Evangelicalism* (New York: Oxford University Press, 2008) and David Domke and Kevin Coe, *The God Strategy: How Religion Became a Political Weapon in America*, 2nd ed. (New York: Oxford University Press, 2010), https://doi.org/10.1093/acprof:oso/9780195326413.001.0001.

may be what is contributing to the destabilization of institutional Christianity.[49] In other words, what may be turning people away from Christ or institutional religion in general is Christianity's (particularly evangelicalism's) unquestioning support of one party's political agenda, even if that agenda openly conflicts with the religion's ethical guidelines. It may even be the case that a growing antagonism toward Republicans (outside of the Midwest and South, of course) may result in an equal disdain for Christianity, as well.[50] As Robert Mohler, president of Southern Baptist Theological Seminary, once said about the 2016 Presidential election, "Long term, I'm afraid people are going to remember evangelicals in this election for supporting the unsupportable and defending the absolutely indefensible."[51]

Seybold's article also has significant implications for understanding evangelicalism's continued support for President Donald Trump despite repeatedly violating traditional Christian ethics by him and his administration. From a cultural cognition perspective, these evangelicals appear to be Republican *first* and Christians second because their identity revolves around societal dominance (not Jesus Christ).[52] Hence, eight out of ten Christian believers cite non-religious and non-spiritual goals, such as family happiness, financial security, and successful careers, as the single most important thing they would like to accomplish in life. Of those who listed some type of spiritual growth as a high priority (20%), half cited mundane objectives, such as maintaining faith in God or knowing they are "saved." When asked to identify personal spiritual goals, the majority of Christians (60%) were unable to do so. Of the 40% who identified a spiritual ambition, only 20% of believers could provide a specific goal they would like to achieve, whereas the other 20% simply offered vague concepts and ideas, such as "to become a better Christian" or "to grow spiritually." Very few of the respondents were able or willing to offer more than one spiritual goal, and less than one in five Christians were able to define "spiritual success" beyond a solitary component of personal maturation.[53]

The point is that from Seybold's article, there are good reasons to believe many so-called "evangelicals" are simply self-identified Republicans who claim the title "Christian" because that is the expectation for membership in their socio-political cohort. In reality, however, these groups appear to be only quasi-evangelical,[54] constituting the disaffected portions of white society who feel they must rebel against a system and culture that is progressively eroding their former societal privilege.[55] If this is indeed the case, the "whitelash" occurring in evangelicalism is likely to continue destabilizing institutional Christianity into the foreseeable future.

---

[49] Kevin S. Seybold, "A Cultural Cognition Perspective on Religion Singularity: How Political Identity Influences Religious Affiliation," *Socio-Historical Examination of Religion and Ministry* 1, no. 1 (Spring 2019): 21–28, https://doi.org/10.33929/sherm.2019.vol1.no1.03.

[50] Cf. Gregory A. Boyd, *The Myth of a Christian Nation: How the Quest for Political Power Is Destroying the Church* (Grand Rapids, MI: Zondervan, 2005).

[51] R. Albert Mohler Jr., "Mohler, Jr. Discusses Evangelical Support for Trump" (YouTube video), October 11, 2016, 00:29–01:21, accessed April 6, 2019, youtube.com/watch?v=s6hsLy0dimA&feature=youtu.be.

[52] See for example, Marvin A. McMickle, "Where Have All the Prophets Gone?," *Ashland Theological Journal* 37 (2005): 13–15.

[53] Barna, *Growing True Disciples*, 35–42.

[54] Cf. Stephen J. Nichols, *Jesus Made in America: A Cultural History from the Puritans to* The Passion of the Christ (Downers Grove, IL: InterVarsity Press, 2008), 198–221.

[55] R. R. Reno, "Trumping Evangelicals," *First Things* 262 (April 2016): 3–4.

Scientific Reductionism: A Response to Jack David Eller

In Jack David Eller's response to the religion singularity, "Is the Disintegration of Christianity a Problem—or Even a Surprise?," he argues for methodological naturalism when tracing the current destabilization of institutional Christianity, rejecting what he perceives to be the metaphysical value judgments of Howard's original article. In other words, Eller emphasizes the need for remaining detached from what he believes is the natural evolutionary development of all religions: birth, growth, adaptation, procreation, and death (just like any other biological organism). In the case of the religion singularity, however, death involves the institutional nature of Christianity as opposed to the religion itself, which Eller argues is likely to flourish despite Christianity's rapid fragmentation. Using Rodney Stark's notion of a "religious economy" (with some reservation), the breakup of churches and denominations simply means more varieties for religious consumers to choose from. As an anthropologist, Eller views the demise of Christianity as only one phase in a long history of denominational speciation, hybridization, and extinction.[56]

Eller's assessment of the religion singularity implicitly differentiates between the positive sciences and metaphysics when he suggests Howard is experiencing "angst" and "distress" at Christianity's destabilization. Of course, Eller does misread Howard's tone when he presumes he "bemoans" the dramatic paradigm shift presently occurring in Christianity. On the contrary, Howard is quite hopeful that these changes, though they may cause the demise of Christianity's traditional institutional structure, will ultimately help Christians recapture the essence of faith apart from institutional and dogmatic control.[57] In any case, we agree with Eller that the scientific study of religion should rely on empirical data and independent evaluations without an ideological allegiance. We believe that Eller is also correct to suggest that there exist no independent criteria with which to corroborate the accuracy of metaphysical speculations, particularly in relation to the abstract realm of spirituality.[58] Hence, he seeks to reorient the "religion singularity" discussion toward an evolutionary interpretation of the data. Anthropologically, the disintegration of institutional Christianity is no surprise since this has been the evolutionary development of most major religions throughout human history. As Eller succinctly describes it, "There is nothing new happening here."[59]

While Eller is undoubtedly correct in his implied demarcation between science and metaphysics (and he is certainly correct that Christianity, like most other major religions, has always been diverse),[60] there is still the danger of presenting an overly reductionistic explanation for the religion singularity. As Eller writes, "Religions … are not eternal stable entities but are mobile, constructed, and *evolving* things like any natural species."[61] It is true that the democratization of Christianity has contributed to the loss of control by religious authorities, but

---

[56] Jack David Eller, "Is the Disintegration of Christianity a Problem—or Even a Surprise?," *Socio-Historical Examination of Religion and Ministry* 1, no. 1 (Spring 2019): 29–38, https://doi.org/10.33929/sherm.2019.vol1.no1.04.

[57] See for example, Howard, *Paradoxy*, esp. 138–76.

[58] See James A. Van Slyke, *The Cognitive Science of Religion*, Ashgate Science and Religion (Burlington, VT: Ashgate Publishing, 2011), 25, https://doi.org/10.4324/9781315614809.

[59] Eller, "Is the Disintegration of Christianity a Problem," 30.

[60] See for example, Martin Hengel, *Between Jesus and Paul: Studies in the Earliest History of Christianity*, trans. John Bowden (Philadelphia, PA: Fortress Press, 1983); Pieter J. Lalleman, "Polymorphy of Christ," in *The Apocryphal Acts of John*, ed. Jan N. Bremmer, Studies on the Apocryphal Acts of the Apostles (Kampen: Kok Pharos, 1995), 1:97–118; and Jacob Parappally, "One Jesus – Many Christologies," *Vidyajyoti Journal of Theological Reflection* 61, no. 10 (1997): 708–18.

[61] Eller, "Is the Disintegration of Christianity a Problem," 32; italics in original.

his belief that the religion singularity is simply another by-product of religious evolution is not causally sufficient to explain the phenomenon in its entirety. The difference here is that the religion singularity is unlike anything observed in *any* religious tradition throughout human history, particularly since there has never been anything like the global reach and influence that institutional Christianity has enjoyed for centuries.[62] Presumably, Eller agrees with this assertion when he acknowledges, "Christianity yearned for, and temporarily appeared to achieve, centralization on a scale that no other religion has accomplished."[63] Hence, the singularity phenomenon is unique precisely because Christianity quickly became global and then, even more rapidly, disintegrated into smaller and smaller fragments, though Howard does not believe congregations will shrink into numerous "church[es]-of-one," as Eller argues.[64] Rather, Howard argues that the religion singularity is best defined as the irreversible collapse of *institutional* forms of Christian faith expression, thereby making typical denominational structures and worship centers unsustainable. Because of this collapse, a transformation in how Christians will "be church" and "do church" is inevitable. Thus, the religion singularity is not so much a prediction of things to come but an observation of an era coming to its inevitable end.

Basic anthropological and cultural evolution are certainly dominant factors contributing to Christianity's destabilization, but this does not make the religion singularity universally applicable to all religions. This is especially true considering that most religions throughout history have been geographically isolated and tribally confined to certain people groups (ethnically, culturally, etc.), with or without institutional centralization.[65] Consequently, the splintering effect found in other religions, such as Judaism and Islam, where division occurs sporadically within a parent tradition (e.g. Reformed vs. Orthodox Judaism; Sunni vs. Shi'a Islam), is not the same phenomenon being described by the religion singularity. Here, Eller falls victim to his own ambiguity when he appears to equate the religion *singularity* with religious *diversity*. The two are not the same. With the latter, each religion has had its share of divergent traditions and dogmas that create fairly minor fragmentations within the religion, but the religious paradigm itself stays intact.[66] Yet, the religion singularity specifically describes such an extreme acceleration of religious division to the point that the entire religion begins to destabilize, ultimately risking total disintegration as a result. To make this distinction even clearer, compare the small handful of Jewish "denominations" that exist in the world today with the estimated 45,000 Christian denominations in 2014.[67] The difference is staggering in terms of sheer numbers, which should prevent any mistaken notion that the religion singularity is also occurring in other religions.

---

[62] See Rodney Stark, *The Triumph of Christianity: How the Jesus Movement Became the World's Largest Religion* (New York: HarperOne, 2011) and Bart D. Ehrman, *The Triumph of Christianity: How a Forbidden Religion Swept the World* (New York: Simon and Schuster, 2018).

[63] Eller, "Is the Disintegration of Christianity a Problem," 32.

[64] Cf. Eller, "Is the Disintegration of Christianity a Problem," 31 and Howard, "The Religion Singularity," 81–86.

[65] E. Geoffrey Parrinder, "Religion: Nature and Origins," in *Companion Encyclopedia of Geography: The Environment and Humankind*, ed. Ian Douglas, Richard Huggett, and Mike Robinson (New York: Routledge, 1996), 120–36, http://dx.doi.org/10.4324/9780203416822.

[66] Cf. Charles B. Jones, "The Necessity of Religious Diversity," *Studies in Religion/Sciences Religieuses* 28, no. 4 (1999): 403–17, http://dx.doi.org/10.1177/000842989902800401.

[67] Howard, "The Religion Singularity," 82.

Furthermore, natural evolutionary development in culture and society may not be causally sufficient to describe the current religion singularity precisely because religious belief is not always a by-product of incremental or social adaptations.[68] In this case, Christianity's fragmentation is actually outpacing cultural and societal evolution. Eller's position appears to be that given enough time, other religions (e.g. Islam) will experience the same speciation, hybridization, and fragmentation as Christianity today. The problem with this reductionistic approach is that institutional Christianity's singularity collapse will undoubtedly impact the spread of other religions and may even initiate inter-cultural revolutions within other traditions *before* they have a chance to reach the same divisive acceleration as Christianity. Likewise, Christianity's rapid global spread occurred in sync with Western colonialism and at a time when non-belief was still socially abhorrent. Non-belief (e.g. atheism, agnosticism, etc.) is becoming more socially acceptable, which will potentially affect other faiths, such as the spread of Islam in non-Muslim countries. Thus, other religions will likely never benefit from colonialism or the near-total acceptance of religion and, therefore, may never reach the same acceleratory phase as Christianity did in the twentieth century. In other words, the kind of evolution happening to institutional Christianity has probably never happened before and may, in fact, never happen again. What social scientists are witnessing is a type of biological *emergence* in which mere evolution is an insufficient explanation.[69]

Ultimately, Eller's contention that "all things evolve, and all things pass" is not causally sufficient to explain the religion singularity.[70] Church growth and decline is simply much more complex than being the by-product of speciation, hybridization, and extinction, particularly when considering factors such as birth rates, youth retention, ministry innovation, types of external operations, institutional allegiances within society, and conflict management.[71] Rather than simply declare that because religion is man-made it must be susceptible to evolutionary change, the religion singularity suggests that institutional Christianity is not as linear in its development as might be expected. Rather than eliminate evolutionary explanations altogether, however, the singularity phenomenon acts as a corrective to overly reductionistic viewpoints about religious growth and change.

Of course, Dr. Eller is absolutely correct that religion, like any other organism, is in a constant state of dynamic flux. Speciation, hybridization, and extinction are just as much a part of religion as they are for the animal kingdom. What is especially interesting is the notion that institutional Christianity has seen both gradual adaptation throughout church history, changing its identity incrementally over time, as well as some forms of punctuated equilibrium where sudden mutations have resulted in dramatic alterations.[72] In every case, there is a process of

[68] See Alicia Juarrero, *Dynamics in Action: Intentional Behavior as a Complex System* (Cambridge, MA: The MIT Press, 1999), 75–128, http://dx.doi.org/10.7551/mitpress/2528.001.0001.

[69] Although, this is not to affirm, as Eller rightly implies, a metaphysical or theological explanation, either, *contra* for example, Max Scheler, *Man's Place in Nature*, trans. Hans Meyerhoff (Boston: Noonday Press, 1961).

[70] Eller, "Is the Disintegration of Christianity a Problem," 36.

[71] See the confluence of numerous sociological factors revealed in Michael Hout, Andrew Greeley, and Melissa J. Wilde, "The Demographic Imperative in Religious Change in the United States," *American Journal of Sociology* 107, no. 2 (September 2001): 468–500, https://doi.org/10.1086/324189; Haskell, Flatt, and Burgoyne, "Theology Matters," 516–17; Finke and Stark, *The Churching of America*, 235–83; and Tamney and Johnson, "The Popularity of Strict Churches," 209–23; Marler and Hadaway, "New Church Development," 47–86; Greer, "Strategies for Evangelism and Growth," 87–111; and Green and Light, "Growth and Decline in an Inclusive Denomination," 112–26.

[72] The sudden appearance and spread of the Church of Jesus Christ of Latter-day Saints ("Mormons") is an example of this punctuated equilibrium in religion.

cross-pollination between religious institutions and the surrounding culture, including other religious institutions and philosophies.[73]

In this sense, Eller is right that nothing new is happening. Christianity was itself a fragmentation from Second Temple (apocalyptic) Judaism and has continued to fragment internally for twenty centuries. The difference, once again, is that Christianity's current religion singularity is more akin to the plant pathogen, hammerhead viroids, than it is to Mammalia. In fact, the religion singularity more aptly correlates to a virus or bacterium, which mutates and evolves at incredible speeds; and like other viruses and bacteria, the rate of mutation is so self-destructively prolific that it has the potential to kill both the virus and the host body.[74] What Eller fails to acknowledge is that this self-destructiveness is not just cultural evolution over time; it is an out of control acceleration of mutations within institutional Christianity.

Moral Failure: A Response to Brian McLaren

According to much sociological research, nonbelievers see Christians as rationalizing their own sense of superiority, which Christians feel gives them permission to behave in an unempathetic and uncompassionate way toward others. While pronouncing a moral judgment on others, Christians (for many) have developed an attitude of judgmentalism where they actually gain satisfaction in pointing out other people's failures.[75] Indeed, the vast majority of younger generations (87%) view Christians today as self-righteous and hyper-judgmental. As a result, the misanthropic appearance of Christian condemnations has caused the church to lose an entire generation of would-be believers.[76] In fact, only 32% of nonChristians have a positive view of self-described born-again believers and only 22% have a positive view of white self-described evangelicals.[77] These perceptions have some basis in fact since studies demonstrate that the more religious people are, the more intolerant they become of differing viewpoints.[78] Sadly, one study even showed a correlation between a family's religiosity and the lack of altruistic, prosocial behavior in children. The more religious the household, the less empathetic

---

[73] See for example, Douglas E. Oakman, "Culture, Society, and Embedded Religion in Antiquity," *Biblical Theology Bulletin* 35, no. 1 (2005): 4–12, http://dx.doi.org/10.1177/01461079050350010201.

[74] Selma Gago et al., "Extremely High Mutation Rate of a Hammerhead Viroid," *Science* 323, no. 5919 (2009): 1308, http://dx.doi.org/10.1126/science.1169202; Rok Krašovec et al., "Spontaneous Mutation Rate Is a Plastic Trait Associated with Population Density Across Domains of Life," *PLOS Biology* 15, no. 8 (2017): e2002731, https://doi.org/10.1371/journal.pbio.2002731.

[75] Cf. Caroline J. Simon, "Judgmentalism," *Faith and Philosophy* 6, no. 3 (1989): 275–87, http://dx.doi.org/10.5840/faithphil19896322.

[76] See the entire discussion in David Kinnaman and Gabe Lyons, *Unchristian: What a New Generation Really Thinks About Christianity ...And Why It Matters* (Grand Rapids, MI: Baker Books, 2007), 181–204.

[77] Sider, *The Scandal of the Evangelical Conscience*, 28.

[78] See Clyde Wilcox and Ted Jelen, "Evangelicals and Political Tolerance," *American Politics Quarterly* 18, no. 1 (January 1990): 25–46, https://doi.org/10.1177/1532673x9001800102; Robert D. Woodberry and Christian Smith, "Fundamentalism et al: Conservative Protestants in America," *Annual Review of Sociology* 24, no. 1 (1998): 25–56, https://doi.org/10.1146/annurev.soc.24.1.25; Samuel H. Reimer and Jerry Z. Park, "Tolerant (In)civility? A Longitudinal Analysis of White Conservative Protestants' Willingness to Grant Civil Liberties," *Journal for the Scientific Study of Religion* 40, no. 4 (December 2001): 735–45, https://doi.org/10.1111/0021-8294.00088; and David P. Gushee, *The Future of Faith in American Politics: The Public Witness of the Evangelical Center* (Waco, TX: Baylor University Press, 2008), 141–74.

and sensitive children were to issues of social injustice. Children in nonreligious households, on the other hand, showed higher degrees of altruism and empathy for the plight of others.[79] Oftentimes, this judgmentalism and social apathy is justified under the pretense of wanting to call attention to the dangers of sin. In reality, however, Christian claims of benevolence ("hating the sin but loving the sinner") merely mask the fault-finder's own hypocrisy.[80] McLaren notes as much elsewhere, "[Evangelical] activists may use the word 'love' to justify their behavior, but those who disagree with them are seldom treated with love."[81]

Significantly, the Buddhist principal of interdependence directly relates to a non-judgmental disposition whereby Buddhist ethics emphasize acceptance and compassion without overt moral condemnation of individuals, which leads directly to Brian McLaren's article, "Conditions for the Great Religion Singularity."[82] Here, McLaren employs the Buddhist "law of interdependent origination" to discuss ten factors that have led to institutional Christianity's religion singularity, including a history of unacknowledged atrocities, scandals, white supremacy, and an overall moral failure in the religion's leaders.[83] These factors in large part reveal that it would be hypocritical for present-day Christians to be judgmental toward others. According to Ron Sider's research, "Born-again Christians divorce at about the same rate as everyone else. Self-centered materialism is seducing evangelicals and rapidly destroying our earlier, slightly more generous giving. Only 6 percent of born-again Christians tithe. Born-again Christians justify and engage in sexual promiscuity (both premarital sex and adultery) at astonishing rates. Racism and perhaps physical abuse of wives seem to be worse in evangelical circles than elsewhere. This is scandalous behavior for people who claim to be born-again by the Holy Spirit."[84] Moreover, a significant number of conservative white evangelicals believe African Americans are naturally lazy and unintelligent. A significant percentage of white evangelicals also oppose laws that protect minorities and are more likely to object to having neighbors of a different race than the general population.[85] As McLaren writes, the moral failure of Christians and Christians leaders "has made claims of one religion's spiritual supremacy over others literally incredible and ethically reprehensible."[86] When taken together, McLaren is right

---

[79] Jean Decety et al., "The Negative Association between Religiousness and Children's Altruism Across the World," *Current Biology* 25, no. 22 (2015): 2951–55, http://dx.doi.org/10.1016/j.cub.2015.09.056.

[80] Cf. David A. Spieler, "Hypocrisy: An Exploration of a 'Third Type'," *Andrews University Seminary Studies* 13, no. 2 (1975): 273–79.

[81] Brian D. McLaren, *A New Kind of Christianity: Ten Questions That Are Transforming the Faith*, Pbk. ed. (New York: HarperCollins, 2011), 174.

[82] See Sallie B. King, "Buddhist Ethics: Engagement without Judgmentalism," *Bridges* 13, no. 3/4 (2006): 287–307. On a personal note, it is quite flattering for McLaren to refer to the phenomenon as "The Great Religion Singularity," an apparent homage to Phyllis Tickle's work, *The Great Emergence* (Phyllis Tickle, *The Great Emergence: How Christianity is Changing and Why* [Grand Rapids, MI: Baker Books, 2008]).

[83] Brian D. McLaren, "Conditions for the Great Religion Singularity," *Socio-Historical Examination of Religion and Ministry* 1, no. 1 (Spring 2019): 40–49, https://doi.org/10.33929/sherm.2019.vol1.no1.05.

[84] Sider, *The Scandal of the Evangelical Conscience*, 27–28.

[85] See the statistics in Robert P. Jones, Daniel Cox, and Rachel Lienesch, *Who Sees Discrimination? Attitudes on Sexual Orientation, Gender Identity, Race, and Immigration Status: Findings from PRRI's American Values Atlas* (Washington, DC: PRRI, 2017), accessed April 5, 2018, https://www.prri.org/research/americans-views-discrimination-immigrants-blacks-lgbt-sex-marriage-immigration-reform/; Sider, *The Scandal of the Evangelical Conscience*, 24–26; Christian Smith, *Christian America? What Evangelicals Really Want* (Berkeley, CA: University of California Press, 2000), 209–12, 221–22; Douglas R. Sharp, "Evangelicals, Racism, and the Limits of Social Science Research," *Christian Scholar's Review* 33, no. 2 (Winter 2004): 240–45; and Michael O. Emerson and Christian Smith, *Divided by Faith: Evangelical Religion and the Problem of Race in America*, Pbk. ed. (New York: Oxford University Press, 2001), esp. 69–91.

[86] McLaren, "Conditions for the Great Religion Singularity," 41.

to hypothesize it is the church's reluctance to change and reluctance to address its own moral failures that has led (in part) to the destabilization of institutional Christianity.

With regards to the other conditions that McLaren identifies, they are exceptionally accurate and well-articulated. However, we would argue for more nuance in his observation about "authoritarian centralization." Rather than see the consolidation of ecclesial power as a cause *for* the religion singularity, it might be more accurate to view the singularity phenomenon as the inevitable reaction *to* this consolidation. The more ecclesial authorities attempt to maintain control, the more institutional Christianity fragments. Likewise, McLaren's "military imperialism," where emperors once used violence to convert the Roman Empire, is reminiscent of earlier patristic writers who continually aligned their faith with the thought processes of the Empire, further solidifying the link between religion and culture. Both conditions contributed to, if not outright exasperated, the change-averse nature of current institutional paradigms, which has become the defining characteristic of the religion singularity.

Conclusion

Overall, the reception and interaction with Ken Howard's article, "The Religion Singularity," has been both positive and informative. From Branch's essay, readers learn of the epistemic foundations that may have contributed to the rapid fragmentation of institutional Christianity. From Lingelbach, readers discover the diversity present in the primitive church, indicating that diversity and fragmentation have been a part of Christianity's history since the beginning. Seybold's article reveals an apparent direct correlation between the polarization of American politics and the disintegration of the church. Eller's article explains the importance of recognizing the natural evolutionary processes of speciation, hybridization, and extinction inherent to all religious belief systems. Finally, with McLaren's article, readers come to understand how institutional Christianity's failure to live up to its own ethical norms undermines its long-term viability. In each essay, the author presents a different perspective for how or why the religion singularity is a present reality in the church today.

As it relates to the religion singularity phenomenon directly, the actual factors that cause a particular church or whole denomination to grow (or decline) are, in reality, a complex system of interrelated congregational personalities and characteristics, such as the ability to retain a strong youth membership, innovative and joyful services, a robust focus on evangelism and charity, support for interreligious dialogue, and the belief that God is active in the life of the congregation.[87] In fact, one study reveals that conservative denominations tend to have higher birth rates where female congregants produced more children at younger ages, thereby accounting for much of evangelical membership in decades past. The same study shows that other factors play a role, such as the fact that conservative conversions to mainline groups have diminished while apostasy rates have increased among liberals.[88]

---

[87] See for example, Haskell, Flatt, and Burgoyne, "Theology Matters," 516–17; Finke and Stark, *The Churching of America*, 235–83; and Tamney and Johnson, "The Popularity of Strict Churches," 209–23. Cf. Thomas and Olson, "Testing the Strictness Thesis," 619–39.

[88] Hout, Greeley, and Wilde, "The Demographic Imperative in Religious Change," 468–500. See also, Hadaway and Marler, "Growth and Decline in the Mainline," 20.

Ultimately, congregations that grow numerically display stronger institutional allegiances, promote a clearer sense of purpose, and emphasize mutual responsibility of evangelistic efforts among their members. They tend to avoid or at least quickly resolve, internal conflict among its members, and have an overall fervent determination to flourish as a church. Likewise, older congregations fail to assimilate new members into their established systems, making younger churches more likely to grow than their older equivalents. Nonetheless, a congregation's eventual growth depends significantly, if not almost entirely, on the socio-economic demographics of its surrounding environment, as well as its outward focus toward the community.[89] In other words, the most predominant factor for predicting church growth is socioeconomic advantages and outreach. With access to higher education, reproductive choices and family planning, career opportunities, cost of living increases, and lifestyle choices comes the inevitable drop in birth rates among developed nations. Liberal denominations suffered the biggest drop in birth rates largely due to their members' educational and social achievements. At the same time, conservative churches have more effectively indoctrinated their children to maintain their religious tradition even into adulthood, as well as "training" their congregants to proselytize more than their liberal counterparts.[90] The point is that numerous socio-political and economic changes in Western culture (and eventually the entire world) have contributed to the growth and decline of individual congregations over the last century, whereas before they were more stable. When compounded over just a few generations, these factors soon intensified to proliferate the rapid increase in both denominations and worship centers. The inevitable result is the "religion singularity." What now remains to be seen is whether and how institutional Christianity will adapt to this change and in what form (if any) it will survive.

BIBLIOGRAPHY

Ahlstrom, Sydney E. *A Religious History of the American People*. New Have, CT: Yale University Press, 1972.

Barna, George. *Growing True Disciples: New Strategies for Producing Genuine Followers of Christ*. Colorado Springs, CO: WaterBrook Press, 2001.

Bass, Diana Butler. *Christianity After Religion: The End of Church and the Birth of a New Spiritual Awakening*. New York: HarperCollins Publishers, 2012.

———. *The Practicing Congregation: Imagining a New Old Church*. Herndon, VA: Alban Institute, 2004.

Bivins, Jason C. *Religion of Fear: The Politics of Horror in Conservative Evangelicalism*. New York: Oxford University Press, 2008.

Bowen, Kurt. *Christians in a Secular World: The Canadian Experience*. Montreal, Quebec: McGill-Queen's University Press, 2004.

Boyarin, Daniel. *Border Lines: The Partition of Judaeo-Christianity*. Philadelphia, PA: University of Pennsylvania Press, 2004. https://doi.org/10.9783/9780812203844.

Boyd, Gregory A. *The Myth of a Christian Nation: How the Quest for Political Power Is Destroying the Church*. Grand Rapids, MI: Zondervan, 2005.

Branch, Jeshua B. "Grenz and Franke's Post-Foundationalism and the Religion Singularity." *Socio-Historical Examination of Religion and Ministry* 1, no. 1 (Spring 2019): 1–9, https://doi.org/10.33929/sherm.2019.vol1.no1.01.

---

[89] See the seven analyses of congregational growth and decline in David A. Roozen and C. Kirk Hadaway, eds., *Church and Denominational Growth* (Nashville, TN: Abingdon Press, 1993), 135–240.

[90] See Hadaway and Marler, "Growth and Decline in the Mainline," 1–24.

Chaves, Mark. *American Religion: Contemporary Trends*. Princeton, NJ: Princeton University Press, 2011. https://doi.org/10.23943/princeton/9780691146850.001.0001.

Cooperman, Alan. *Choosing a New Church or House of Worship: Americans Look for Good Sermons, Warm Welcome*. Washington, DC: Pew Research Center, Aug. 23, 2016. Accessed April 3, 2019. https://www.pewforum.org/2016/08/23/choosing-a-new-church-or-house-of-worship/.

de Boer, Martinus C. "The Nazoreans: Living at the Boundary of Judaism and Christianity." In *Tolerance and Intolerance in Early Judaism and Christianity*, edited by Graham N. Stanton and Guy G. Stroumsa, 239–62. New York: Cambridge University Press, 1998. http://dx.doi.org/10.1017/cbo9780511659645.015.

Decety, Jean, Jason M. Cowell, Kang Lee, Randa Mahasneh, Susan Malcolm-Smith, Bilge Selcuk, and Xinyue Zhou. "The Negative Association between Religiousness and Children's Altruism Across the World." *Current Biology* 25, no. 22 (2015): 2951–55. http://dx.doi.org/10.1016/j.cub.2015.09.056.

Doane, A. N. "The Ethnography of Scribal Writing and Anglo-Saxon Poetry: Scribe as Performer." *Oral Tradition* 9, no. 2 (October 1994): 420–39.

Domke, David, and Kevin Coe. *The God Strategy: How Religion Became a Political Weapon in America*. 2nd ed. New York: Oxford University Press, 2010. https://doi.org/10.1093/acprof:oso/9780195326413.001.0001.

Donahue, Michael J., and Peter L. Benson. "Belief Style, Congregational Climate, and Program Quality." In *Church and Denominational Growth*, edited by David A. Roozen and C. Kirk Hadaway, 225–40. Nashville, TN: Abingdon Press, 1993.

Dougherty, Kevin D., Brandon C. Martinez, and Gerardo Martí "Congregational Diversity and Attendance in a Mainline Protestant Denomination." *Journal for the Scientific Study of Religion* 54, no. 4 (December 2015): 668–83. https://doi.org/10.1111/jssr.12229.

Ehrman, Bart D. *The Triumph of Christianity: How a Forbidden Religion Swept the World*. New York: Simon and Schuster, 2018.

Eller, Jack David. "Is the Disintegration of Christianity a Problem—or Even a Surprise?" *Socio-Historical Examination of Religion and Ministry* 1, no. 1 (Spring 2019): 29–38, https://doi.org/10.33929/sherm.2019.vol1.no1.04.

Emerson, Michael O., and Christian Smith. *Divided by Faith: Evangelical Religion and the Problem of Race in America*. 2000. Pbk. ed. New York: Oxford University Press, 2001.

Eve, Eric. *Behind the Gospels: Understanding the Oral Tradition*. 2013. Reprint, Minneapolis, MN: Fortress Press, 2014.

Finke, Roger, and Rodney Stark. *The Churching of America, 1776–2005: Winners and Losers in Our Religious Economy*. New Brunswick, NJ: Rutgers University Press, 2005.

Finnegan, Ruth H. *Literacy and Orality: Studies in the Technology of Communication*. Oxford, England: Basil Blackwell, 1988.

Flatt, Kevin N. *After Evangelicalism: The Sixties and the United Church of Canada*. Montreal, Quebec: McGill-Queen's University Press, 2013.

Foley, John Miles. "Memory in Oral Tradition." In *Performing the Gospel: Orality, Memory, and Mark; Essays Dedicated to Werner Kelber*. Pbk. ed, edited by Richard A. Horsley, Jonathan A. Draper, and John Miles Foley, 83–96. Minneapolis, MN: Fortress Press, 2011.

Gago, Selma, Santiago F. Elena, Ricardo Flores, and Rafael Sanjuán. "Extremely High Mutation Rate of a Hammerhead Viroid." *Science* 323, no. 5919 (March 2009): 1308. http://dx.doi.org/10.1126/science.1169202.

Green, Norman M., and Paul W. Light. "Growth and Decline in an Inclusive Denomination: The ABC Experience." In *Church and Denominational Growth*, edited by David A. Roozen and C. Kirk Hadaway, 112–26. Nashville, TN: Abingdon Press, 1993.

Greer, Bruce A. "Strategies for Evangelism and Growth in Three Denominations (1965–1990)." In *Church and Denominational Growth*, edited by David A. Roozen and C. Kirk Hadaway, 87–111. Nashville, TN: Abingdon Press, 1993.

Gushee, David P. *The Future of Faith in American Politics: The Public Witness of the Evangelical Center.* Waco, TX: Baylor University Press, 2008.

Hadaway, C. Kirk. "Is Evangelistic Activity Related to Church Growth?" In *Church and Denominational Growth*, edited by David A. Roozen and C. Kirk Hadaway, 169–87. Nashville, TN: Abingdon Press, 1993.

Hadaway, C. Kirk, and Penny Long Marler. "Growth and Decline in the Mainline." In *Faith in America: Changes, Challenges, New Directions*, edited by Charles H. Lippy. Vol. 1, *Organized Religion Today*, 1–24. Westport, CT: Praeger Publishers, 2006.

Halbwachs, Maurice. *On Collective Memory*. Edited and translated by Lewis A. Coser. Chicago, IL: University of Chicago Press, 1992.

Haskell, David Millard, Kevin N. Flatt, and Stephanie Burgoyne. "Theology Matters: Comparing the Traits of Growing and Declining Mainline Protestant Church Attendees and Clergy." *Review of Religious Research* 58, no. 4 (2016): 515–41. http://dx.doi.org/10.1007/s13644-016-0255-4.

Hengel, Martin. *Between Jesus and Paul: Studies in the Earliest History of Christianity*. Translated by John Bowden. Philadelphia, PA: Fortress Press, 1983.

Hout, Michael, Andrew Greeley, and Melissa J. Wilde. "The Demographic Imperative in Religious Change in the United States." *American Journal of Sociology* 107, no. 2 (September 2001): 468–500. https://doi.org/10.1086/324189.

Howard, Kenneth W. *Excommunicating the Faithful: Jewish Christianity in the Early Church*. 3rd ed. Germantown, MD: FaithX Press, 2013.

———. *Paradoxy: Creating Christian Community Beyond Us and Them*. Brewster, MA: Paraclete Press, 2010.

———. "The Religion Singularity: A Demographic Crisis Destabilizing and Transforming Institutional Christianity." *International Journal of Religion and Spirituality in Society* 7, no. 2 (2017): 77–93. http://dx.doi.org/10.18848/2154-8633/cgp/v07i02/77-93.

Huebenthal, Sandra. "Social and Cultural Memory in Biblical Exegesis: The Quest for an Adequate Application." In *Cultural Memory in Biblical Exegesis*, edited by Pernille Carstens, Trine Hasselbalch, and Niels Peter Lemche. Perspectives on Hebrew Scriptures and Its Contexts 17, 175–99. Piscataway, NJ: Gorgias Press, 2012.

Johnson, Phil. "You Can't Handle the Truth: The Sinful Tolerance of Postmodernism." *The Journal of Modern Ministry* 1, no. 2 (Fall 2004): 219–45.

Jones, Charles B. "The Necessity of Religious Diversity." *Studies in Religion/Sciences Religieuses* 28, no. 4 (1999): 403–17. http://dx.doi.org/10.1177/000842989902800401.

Jones, Robert P. *The End of White Christian America*. New York: Simon and Schuster Paperbacks, 2016.

Jones, Robert P., Daniel Cox, and Rachel Lienesch. *Who Sees Discrimination? Attitudes on Sexual Orientation, Gender Identity, Race, and Immigration Status: Findings from PRRI's American Values Atlas*. Washington, DC: PRRI, 2017. Accessed April 5, 2018. https://www.prri.org/research/americans-views-discrimination-immigrants-blacks-lgbt-sex-marriage-immigration-reform/.

Juarrero, Alicia. *Dynamics in Action: Intentional Behavior as a Complex System*. Cambridge, MA: The MIT Press, 1999. http://dx.doi.org/10.7551/mitpress/2528.001.0001.

Kelber, Werner H. "In the Beginning Were the Words: The Apotheosis and Narrative Displacement of the Logos." In *Imprints, Voiceprints, and Footprints of Memory: Collected Essays of Werner h. Kelber*. Resources for Biblical Study, 75–102. Atlanta, GA: SBL Press, 2013. http://dx.doi.org/10.2307/j.ctt5hjh34.10.

King, Sallie B. "Buddhist Ethics: Engagement without Judgmentalism." *Bridges* 13, no. 3 (2006): 287–307.

Kinnaman, David, and Gabe Lyons. *Unchristian: What a New Generation Really Thinks About Christianity ...And Why It Matters*. Grand Rapids, MI: Baker Books, 2007.

Kirk, Alan. "Manuscript Tradition as A *Tertium Quid*: Orality and Memory in Scribal Practices." In *Memory and the Jesus Tradition: The Reception of Jesus in the First Three Centuries*, 114–37. New York: Bloomsbury T&T Clark, 2018. http://dx.doi.org/10.5040/9780567663474.0014.

———. "Social and Cultural Memory." In *Memory, Tradition, and Text: Use of the Past in Early Christianity*, edited by Alan Kirk and Tom Thatcher. Semeia Studies 52, 1–24. Boston, MA: SBL, 2005.

Koester, Craig R. "The Origin and Significance of the Flight to Pella Tradition." *The Catholic Biblical Quarterly* 51, no. 1 (January 1989): 90–106.

Kohut, Andrew, Scott Keeter, Carroll Doherty, and Michael Dimock. *Some Social Conservative Disillusionment: More Americans Question Religion's Role in Politics* (Results from the 2008 Annual Religion and Public Life Survey). Washington, DC: Pew Research Center, August 21, 2008. Accessed April 6, 2019. http://assets.pewresearch.org/wp-content/uploads/sites/5/legacy-pdf/445.pdf.

Krašovec, Rok, Huw Richards, Danna R. Gifford, Charlie Hatcher, Katy J. Faulkner, Roman V. Belavkin, Alastair Channon, Elizabeth Aston, Andrew J. McBain, and Christopher G. Knight. "Spontaneous Mutation Rate Is a Plastic Trait Associated with Population Density Across Domains of Life." *PLOS Biology* 15, no. 8 (2017): e2002731. https://doi.org/10.1371/journal.pbio.2002731.

Lalleman, Pieter J. "Polymorphy of Christ." In *The Apocryphal Acts of John*, edited by Jan N. Bremmer. Vol. 1. Studies on the Apocryphal Acts of the Apostles, 97–118. Kampen: Kok Pharos, 1995.

Lingelbach, John F. "First Century Christian Diversity: Historical Evidence of a Social Phenomenon." *Socio-Historical Examination of Religion and Ministry* 1, no. 1 (Spring 2019): 11–20, https://doi.org/10.33929/sherm.2019.vol1.no1.02.

Lord, Albert B. *The Singer of Tales*. 2nd ed. Edited by Stephen Mitchell and Gregory Nagy. Cambridge, MA: Harvard University Press, 2000.

Lugo, Luis. *U.S. Religious Landscape Survey: Religious Affiliation; Diverse and Dynamic*. Washington, DC: Pew Research Center, Feb. 2008. Accessed April 3, 2019. https://www.pewforum.org/2008/02/01/u-s-religious-landscape-survey-religious-affiliation/.

MacArthur, John F. Jr. *The Truth War: Fighting for Certainty in an Age of Deception*. Nashville, TN: Thomas Nelson, 2007.

March, Jennifer. "Reconsidering Mainline Decline: Contemporary Forms of Mainline Adaptation and Congregational Survival." Paper presented at the annual meeting of the American Sociological Association, Montreal, Quebec, 2006.

Marler, Penny Long, and C. Kirk Hadaway. "New Church Development and Denominational Growth (1950–1988): Symptom or Cause?" In *Church and Denominational Growth*, edited by David A. Roozen and C. Kirk Hadaway, 47–86. Nashville, TN: Abingdon Press, 1993.

McLaren, Brian D. "Conditions for the Great Religion Singularity." *Socio-Historical Examination of Religion and Ministry* 1, no. 1 (2019): 40–49, https://doi.org/10.33929/sherm.2019.vol1.no1.05.

———. *A New Kind of Christianity: Ten Questions That Are Transforming the Faith*. Pbk. ed. New York: HarperCollins, 2011.

McMickle, Marvin A. "Where Have All the Prophets Gone?" *Ashland Theological Journal* 37 (2005): 7–18.

Mimouni, S. C. "Les nazoréens: Recherche étymologique et historique." *Revue Biblique* 105, no. 2 (1998): 208–62.

Mohler, R. Albert Jr. "Mohler, Jr. Discusses Evangelical Support for Trump" (YouTube video). October 11, 2016. Accessed April 6, 2019. youtube.com/watch?v=s6hsLy0dimA&feature=youtu.be.

Nichols, Stephen J. *Jesus Made in America: A Cultural History from the Puritans to* The Passion of the Christ. Downers Grove, IL: InterVarsity Press, 2008.

O'Keeffe, Katherine O'Brien. *Visible Song: Transitional Literacy in Old English Verse.* New York: Cambridge University Press, 1990.

Oakman, Douglas E. "Culture, Society, and Embedded Religion in Antiquity." *Biblical Theology Bulletin* 35, no. 1 (2005): 4–12. http://dx.doi.org/10.1177/01461079050350010201.

Olson, Daniel V. A. "Congregational Growth and Decline in Indiana Among Five Mainline Denominations." In *Church and Denominational Growth*, edited by David A. Roozen and C. Kirk Hadaway, 208–24. Nashville, TN: Abingdon Press, 1993.

Ong, Walter J. *Orality and Literacy.* 3rd ed. London: Routledge, 2012. http://dx.doi.org/10.4324/9780203103258.

Pagels, Elaine. *The Gnostic Gospels.* 1979. Pbk. ed. Reprint, New York: Vintage Books, 1989.

Parappally, Jacob. "One Jesus – Many Christologies." *Vidyajyoti Journal of Theological Reflection* 61, no. 10 (1997): 708–18.

Parrinder, E. Geoffrey. "Religion: Nature and Origins." In *Companion Encyclopedia of Geography: The Environment and Humankind*, edited by Ian Douglas, Richard Huggett, and Mike Robinson, 120–36. New York: Routledge, 1996. http://dx.doi.org/10.4324/9780203416822.

Person, Raymond F. Jr. "The Ancient Israelite Scribe as Performer." *Journal of Biblical Literature* 117, no. 4 (Winter 1998): 601–9. http://dx.doi.org/10.2307/3266629.

Reimer, Samuel H., and Jerry Z. Park. "Tolerant (In)civility? A Longitudinal Analysis of White Conservative Protestants' Willingness to Grant Civil Liberties." *Journal for the Scientific Study of Religion* 40, no. 4 (December 2001): 735–45. https://doi.org/10.1111/0021-8294.00088.

Reno, R. R. "Trumping Evangelicals." *First Things* 262 (April 2016): 3–7.

Robinson, James M., and Helmut Koester. *Trajectories through Early Christianity.* 1971. Reprint, Eugene, OR: Wipf and Stock Publishers, 2006.

Rodríguez, Rafael. *Oral Tradition and the New Testament: A Guide for the Perplexed.* New York: Bloomsbury T&T Clark, 2014. https://doi.org/10.5040/9781472550675.

Scheler, Max. *Man's Place in Nature.* Translated by Hans Meyerhoff. Boston: Noonday Press, 1961.

Seybold, Kevin S. "A Cultural Cognition Perspective on Religion Singularity: How Political Identity Influences Religious Affiliation." *Socio-Historical Examination of Religion and Ministry* 1, no. 1 (2019): 21–28, https://doi.org/10.33929/sherm.2019.vol1.no1.03.

Sider, Ronald J. *The Scandal of the Evangelical Conscience: Why Are Christians Living Just Like the Rest of the World?* Grand Rapids, MI: Baker Books, 2005.

Simon, Caroline J. "Judgmentalism." *Faith and Philosophy* 6, no. 3 (1989): 275–87. http://dx.doi.org/10.5840/faithphil19896322.

Sharp, Douglas R. "Evangelicals, Racism, and the Limits of Social Science Research." *Christian Scholar's Review* 33, no. 2 (Winter 2004): 237–61.

Slade, Darren M. "Miracle Eyewitness Reports." In *Encyclopedia of Psychology and Religion*, edited by David A. Leeming, 1. Berlin, Heidelberg: Springer, 2018. http://dx.doi.org/10.1007/978-3-642-27771-9_200227-1.

———. "Religious Homophily and Biblicism: A Theory of Conservative Church Fragmentation." *The International Journal of Religion and Spirituality in Society* 9, no. 1 (2019): 13–28. http://dx.doi.org/10.18848/2154-8633/cgp/v09i01/13-28.

Smith, Christian. *Christian America? What Evangelicals Really Want.* Berkeley, CA: University of California Press, 2000.

Smith, Gregory. *America's Changing Religious Landscape: Christians Decline Sharply as Share of Population; Unaffiliated and Other Faiths Continue to Grow.* Washington, DC: Pew Research Center, May 12, 2015. Accessed April 3, 2019. https://www.pewforum.org/2015/05/12/americas-changing-religious-landscape/.

Spieler, David A. "Hypocrisy: An Exploration of a 'Third Type'." *Andrews University Seminary Studies* 13, no. 2 (1975): 273–79.

Stark, Rodney. *The Triumph of Christianity: How the Jesus Movement Became the World's Largest Religion*. New York: HarperOne, 2011.

———. *What Americans Really Believe: New Findings from the Baylor Surveys of Religion*. Waco, TX: Baylor University Press, 2008.

Stark, Rodney, and Roger Finke. *Acts of Faith: Explaining the Human Side of Religion*. Berkeley, CA: University of California Press, 2000.

Tamney, Joseph B., and Stephen D. Johnson. "The Popularity of Strict Churches." *Review of Religious Research* 39, no. 3 (March 1998): 209–23. https://doi.org/10.2307/3512589.

Taylor, Joan E. "The Phenomenon of Early Jewish-Christianity: Reality or Scholarly Invention?" *Vigiliae Christianae* 44, no. 4 (1990): 313–34. http://dx.doi.org/10.1163/157007290x00090.

Tellbe, Mikael. "De Efesoskristna : Teologisk mångfald och social identitet i den tidiga kristna rörelsen." *Svensk Teologisk Kvartalskrift* 86, no. 1 (2010): 4–12.

Thomas, Jeremy N., and Daniel V. A. Olson. "Testing the Strictness Thesis and Competing Theories of Congregational Growth." *Journal for the Scientific Study of Religion* 49, no. 4 (December 2010): 619–39. https://doi.org/10.1111/j.1468-5906.2010.01534.x.

Tickle, Phyllis. *The Great Emergence: How Christianity is Changing and Why*. Grand Rapids, MI: Baker Books, 2008.

Trebilco, Paul. "Christian Communities in Western Asia Minor into the Early Second Century: Ignatius and Others as Witnesses Against Bauer." *Journal of the Evangelical Theological Society* 49, no. 1 (March 2006): 17–44.

Utter, Glenn H., and John W. Storey. *The Religious Right: A Reference Handbook*. 3rd ed. Millerton, NY: Grey House Publishing, 2007.

van Aarde, Andries G. "Ebionite Tendencies in the Jesus Tradition: The Infancy Gospel of Thomas Interpreted from the Perspective of Ethnic Identity." *Neotestamentica* 40, no. 2 (2006): 353–82.

van Houwelingen, P. H. R. "Fleeing Forward: The Departure of Christians from Jerusalem to Pella." *The Westminster Theological Journal* 65, no. 2 (Fall 2003): 181–200.

Van Slyke, James A. *The Cognitive Science of Religion*. Ashgate Science and Religion. Burlington, VT: Ashgate Publishing, 2011. https://doi.org/10.4324/9781315614809.

Wilcox, Clyde, and Ted Jelen. "Evangelicals and Political Tolerance." *American Politics Quarterly* 18, no. 1 (January 1990): 25–46. https://doi.org/10.1177/1532673x9001800102.

Woodberry, Robert D., and Christian Smith. "Fundamentalism et al: Conservative Protestants in America." *Annual Review of Sociology* 24, no. 1 (1998): 25–56. https://doi.org/10.1146/annurev.soc.24.1.25.

ABOUT THE AUTHORS

Darren M. Slade is a theological historian, systematician, and critical rationalist philosopher from Denver, Colorado. Specializing in historic-speculative theology, theoretical metaphysics, and the socio-political development of religious belief systems, Darren's academic publications include investigations into Islamic history, church history, ancient Near-Eastern textual interpretations, and the academic study of the philosophy, sociology, and psychology of religion. He earned his PhD in theology and church history from the Rawlings School of Divinity (Virginia).

Kenneth W. Howard is an author, strategic missional consultant, church demographer, and church futurist from Germantown, Maryland. Ordained as an Episcopal priest and canonically resident in the Episcopal Diocese of Washington, Ken is the founder and executive director of The FaithX Project, a nonprofit consulting and resource development practice serving congregational and judicatory leaders of all faith traditions. Ken is the author of several books and research articles. He holds a Master of Education from Virginia Commonwealth University and a Master of Divinity from Virginia Theological Seminary.

MORE FROM THE AUTHORS

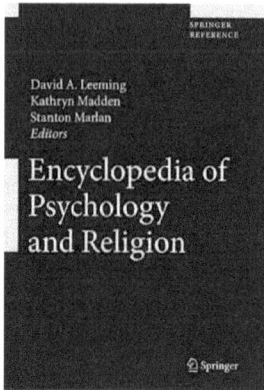

Encyclopedia of Psychology and Religion
(3rd. ed)
(2019, Springer)

Darren M. Slade

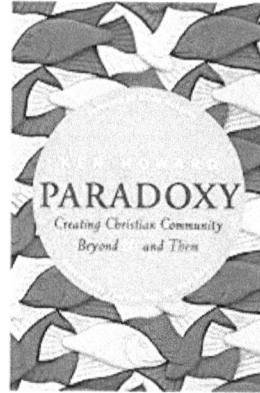

Paradoxy: Creating Christian
Community Beyond Us and Them
(2016, FaithX)

Kenneth W. Howard

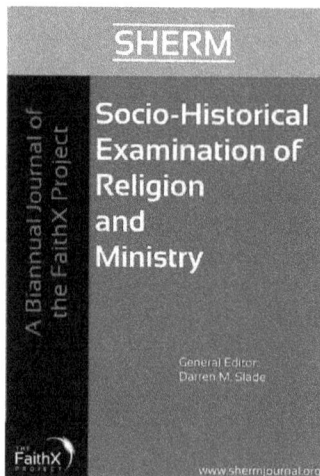

Join host

Robert Johnson

as he explores the intersection of

Freemasonry with culture, religion, politics,

history and *more!*

WCY PODCAST

Whence Came You?

WCY Media LLC

WCYPODCAST.COM

SHERM 1/1 (2019): 76–83

Book Review

Crossing Boundaries, Redefining Faith:
Interdisciplinary Perspectives on the Emerging Church Movement.
Michael Clawson and April Stace, eds.
Eugene, OR: Pickwick Publications, 2016.

Robert D. Francis,
Johns Hopkins University

Abstract: The Emerging Church Movement (ECM) has attracted a surprising amount of scholarly attention for a phenomenon notoriously resistant to definition and whose impact and size have been challenging to quantify. This edited volume, Crossing Boundaries, Redefining Faith: Interdisciplinary Perspectives on the Emerging Church Movement, *seeks to be a touchstone of the best scholarship about the ECM to date. Across ten chapters with thirteen contributors, the volume succeeds, although it is not without its flaws. Most notably, the relatively small universe of congregations upon which the work in this volume—and broader ECM scholarship—is based raises the question of how to quantify the impact and significance of the movement, something this volume leaves unresolved. Nonetheless, there is little doubt that* Crossing Boundaries, Redefining Faith—*as a single volume—is the best assemblage of scholarship about the ECM thus far. This book makes obvious sense as a core text for any college or seminary course.*

Keywords: Emerging Church Movement (ECM), Emerging Church, Ancient-Future, Postmodern, Postcolonial

THE EMERGING CHURCH MOVEMENT (ECM) has attracted a surprising amount of scholarly attention for a phenomenon notoriously resistant to definition and whose impact and size have been challenging to quantify. While this edited volume, *Crossing Boundaries, Redefining Faith: Interdisciplinary Perspectives on the Emerging Church Movement* (hereafter *CBRF*), does not seek to resolve every ambiguity or debate surrounding the ECM, its editors wish for the book to be an interdisciplinary conversation (to borrow a popular ECM term) that can serve as a touchstone on the ECM to date. At least one prominent ECM scholar thinks *CBRF* has succeeded: Josh Packard, author of *The Emerging Church*, declares in the Forward of *CBRF*, "This volume is the pinnacle of academic understanding of the Emerging Church Movement" (xi). Across ten chapters with thirteen contributors, *CBRF* largely succeeds in living up to Packard's claim, although the book is not without its flaws or omissions.

Editors Michael Clawson and April Stace tout the interdisciplinary nature of the volume in its subtitle, a reality born out in its pages. In assembling *CBRF*, the editors enlisted many of the central contributors to ECM scholarship. For example, *CBRF* has entries by Gerardo Marti, James Bielo, and the aforementioned Packard, authors (or coauthor, in the case of Marti) of arguably the three most foundational scholarly books on the ECM.[1] Other contributors include

---

[1] See James S. Bielo, *Emerging Evangelicals: Faith, Modernity, and the Desire for Authenticity* (New York: NYU Press, 2011), https://doi.org/10.18574/nyu/9780814789544.001.0001; Gerardo Marti and Gladys Ganiel, *The Deconstructed Church: Understanding Emerging Christianity* (New York: Oxford University Press, 2014), https://doi.org/10.1093/acprof:oso/9780199959884.001.0001; and Josh Packard, *The Emerging Church: Religion at the Margins*, Religion in Politics and Society (Boulder, CO: First Forum Press, 2012).

Socio-Historical Examination of Religion and Ministry
Volume 1, Issue 1, Spring 2019 www.shermjournal.org
© *Wipf and Stock Publishers. All Rights Reserved.*
Permissions: shermeditor@gmail.com
ISSN 2637-7519 (print), ISSN 2637-7500 (online)
https://doi.org/10.33929/sherm.2019.vol1.no1.07 (article)

WIPF *and*
STOCK
Publishers

an historian, two anthropologists, and several sociologists, as well as scholars of theology, religious studies, and music. In some cases, the contributions to *CBRF* represent original scholarship regarding the ECM, while in others, the author(s) summarize or build upon existing work available elsewhere. In virtually all cases, the contributors have experienced the ECM firsthand, either as a participant observer, practitioner, researcher, or all three.

The chapters are grouped into two main sections. Chapters 1–5, "Defining Boundaries," are concerned with the characteristics of the ECM, no small task for a movement defined in part by its resistance to definitions. Chapters 6–10, "Crossing Boundaries", explore ways the ECM has lived out one of its core intentions, namely revising, reconstructing, and re-envisioning Christian faith. The Introduction by Clawson and Stace, while brief, provides helpful clarity about the ECM and related terms, something vital when dealing with a phenomenon as contested as the ECM. The Introduction pairs well with Chapter 1, in which Clawson sets forward a brief but thorough history of the ECM. Not only do these entries provide a solid foundation, but they are also useful as standalone selections for anyone interested in a primer on the ECM.

The remaining four chapters in the first section include two contributions each from social scientists (Chapters 3 and 4) and theologians (Chapters 4 and 5), although all four entries are based, in one form or another, on social scientific data: ethnographic fieldwork, interviews, or textual analyses of ECM literature. In Chapter 2, sociologist Gerardo Marti—in a contribution that is largely a summary of his book with Gladys Ganiel about the ECM—seeks to "conceptualize a set of core processes inherent to the movement" (47). Using his sociological lens, he identifies the ECM as "built on the continual practice of deconstruction" (46), reacting mainly against conservative Protestantism but also against other forms of staid religion. For Marti, the ECM embodies what he terms "collective religious institutional entrepreneurship." Chapter 3, contributed by anthropologists Jon Bialecki and James Bielo, presents "an ethnographically informed theoretical framework that can accurately apprehend the way Emerging Christians do time" (71), namely "ancient-future" temporality. Perhaps the most theoretical entry of the book, this chapter marries its theoretical sophistication with a visit into actual emerging church space, exploring the practices, images, and symbols employed by one Emerging community in Cincinnati.

Chapters 4 and 5 turn toward the theological, although notably, both authors ground their analyses in interviews, ethnography, and participant observation. In Chapter 4, Xochitl Alvizo—having noticed connections between the ECM and feminist theology—seeks to move past ECM values as proclaimed in its literature in order to assess "the Emerging Church's faithfulness to its own claims about what it is as church" (94). Alvizo uses interviews and textual study of twelve ECM congregations often-referenced in ECM literature "to uncover the ecclesiology practiced and embodied" (94) by these prominent churches. She observes that while the ECM communities she studied do, indeed, cater to those harmed by Christianity, they also largely lack an explicit critique of patriarchy. She concludes by returning to themes in feminist theology, calling on the ECM to continue to live into the fullness of what it professes.

Similarly, Chapter 5 is a theological reflection grounded in fieldwork. In this case, Timothy Snyder first suggests that "the most interesting reality of the movement is its otherness" (121), and then uses a single-site case study of House of Mercy, an Emerging church in Minneapolis, to explore "the *possibility* present" (121) when an unsettled culture (House of Mercy) comes into contact—and conflict—with a settled one (the Evangelical Lutheran Church in America). With his contribution, Snyder seeks to remedy what he says is a lack of attention in ECM scholarship to the ECM's conflict with more conventional forms of Christianity.

Section two of *CBRF*, "Crossing Boundaries", contains five chapters that are also balanced among disciplines, with two chapters from sociologists, two from theologians, and one from a scholar of music. In Chapter 6, sociologist Lloyd Chia explores how the ECM maps itself in relation to others. Primarily using ECM events, books, publications, blogs, and websites (141), Chia argues that the ECM seeks to occupy "Borderlands" (162), spaces in which it can encounter difference. Chia's contribution would have been stronger had it drawn more explicitly on the extensive fieldwork from his dissertation, in which he—like Alvizo in Chapter 4—goes beyond the rhetoric of the ECM to see if it is actually inclusive in its practice.[2] Nonetheless, it is valuable to understand "how the Emerging Church imagines itself in relation to others" (162).

The next three chapters—contributed by a sociologist, theologian, and scholar of music, respectively—fit nicely together given their foci on the practices of Emerging congregations, specifically in the realms of worship and community life. In Chapter 7, sociologist Jason Wollschleger first establishes that the ECM is a "reactionary movement committed to radical authenticity" (166), and then—based upon fieldwork at Church of the Apostles in Seattle—argues that what the ECM is primarily reacting against is the differentiation of social spheres into sacred and secular. April Stace follows in Chapter 8 with an exploration of the use of "popular-secular music" (181) in worship, based upon her fieldwork as participant observer at five ECM congregations in the greater Washington, DC area. Like Wollschleger, Stace emphasizes the discarding of the sacred-secular distinction among the churches she studied; she argues this is not a "secularization" of sacred space, but the reverse: a "'sacralization' of all of life experiences" (189). In Chapter 9, Heather Josselyn-Cranson—a scholar and practitioner of sacred music—seeks to "shed light on worship within the Emerging Church" (192). She hypothesizes that Emerging churches, as communities shaped by postmodernity, should reflect "the inclusive and juxtaposed musical approach" (198) of postmodern music. However, her previous study of three Emerging church congregations in the Midwest found little musical variety; so, for this chapter, she found one that did: a joint congregation, St. Andrew and All Souls, in Portland, Oregon. In her analysis of about six months of services, she found the expected musical diversity—a "messy vitality"—and proposes "five principles of musical variety" (210) for other congregations to consider.

It is fitting—and indeed, necessary—that Clawson and Stace use the final chapter of *CBRF* to counterbalance the book's almost exclusive focus on American ECM. In Chapter 10, theologians Juan José Barreda Toscano and Dee Yaccino explore the ways in which "a Latin American theology of integral mission" (215) has impacted that region and converged with broader trends in Christianity. They begin with the legacy of colonialism, posing the question of what a postmodern theological turn looks like in places "not yet seen as modern" (219). Latin American Emergence, while synergistic with American ECM, must be understood contextually, "in the sense of looking at their own contexts from a postcolonial vantage point" (219). Toscano and Yaccino then document the *Red del Camino*, "a network of churches and ministries committed to the promotion and practices of integral mission at the local church level" (221).

CBRF should be of interest to several audiences. This volume makes obvious sense as a core text for any college or seminary course about the ECM. Further, certain chapters would

---

[2] See Lloyd Chia, "Emerging Faith Boundaries: Bridge-Building, Inclusion, and the Emerging Church Movement in America" (PhD diss., University of Missouri-Columbia, 2010), https://mospace.umsystem.edu/xmlui/bitstream/handle/10355/10278/research.pdf?sequence=3.

be useful in a wide range of other undergraduate or graduate courses across disciplines: social and religious movements, late twentieth and early twenty-first century American Christianity, the sociology or anthropology of religion, feminist theologies, church music, and comparative religion, among others. While scholars of religion should consider adding this volume to their personal collections, interested laypersons might find some chapters more engaging and accessible than others. That said, the Introduction and Chapter 1 would be useful for virtually any reader interested in a thorough treatment of the basic outlines of the ECM and its history. Given the volume's academic bent, pastors and teachers looking to introduce parishioners to ECM teachings or practice are probably better served to look elsewhere, but there is little doubt that—as a single volume—*CBRF* is the best assemblage of scholarship about the ECM to date, even if not every chapter is for every reader.

A single volume of ten chapters can only cover so much ground, so despite the commendable reach and range of contributions, there are a few additional topics that deserve attention in order to give a fuller sense of existing scholarship on the ECM. Concerning the inclusion of nondominant perspectives, while there is an analysis of the ECM from the perspective of feminist theology, discussion of race is conspicuously absent for a movement often critiqued for its whiteness.[3] Similarly, with the notable exception of the final chapter, the volume is almost wholly focused on the ECM within the United States, despite the fact that some of the earliest ECM thinkers and expressions derived from elsewhere, a fact Clawson acknowledges in Chapter 1.[4] Another welcome addition would have been more discussion of the ECM in light of contemporaneous cultural and religious trends—like the rise of religious "nones" and growing disaffection toward the Religious Right—although that has now been addressed in a newly published scholarly collection.[5] Finally, a scholarly treatment of the ECM's entanglements with American politics on both the right and left would have seized upon another long-running debate within the ECM and beyond.[6]

Within sociology, there is a developing critique stating that what people think about poor neighborhoods comes from an oversaturation of research on a few over-studied cities, which happen to host major sociology departments that train ethnographers.[7] A related concern can be raised about scholarship on the ECM, which has had an almost exclusive focus on

---

[3] See for instance, David Fitch, "Why the Missional/Emerging Church is so Young and White," *Missio Alliance* (blog), January 16, 2009, https://www.missioalliance.org/why-the-missionalemerging-church-is-so-young-and-white/; Tony Jones, "How White Is the Emerging Church?," *Theoblogy*, May 8, 2012, https://www.patheos.com/blogs/tonyjones/2012/05/08/how-white-is-the-emerging-church/; Soong-Chan Rah and Jason Mach, "Is the Emerging Church for Whites Only?" *Sojourners Magazine*, May 2010, 16–19.

[4] For an example of a comparative perspective, see Mathew Guest, "The Emerging Church in Transatlantic Perspective," *Journal for the Scientific Study of Religion* 56, no. 1 (March 2017): 41–51, https://doi.org/10.1111/jssr.12326.

[5] Randall Reed and G. Michael Zbaraschuk, *The Emerging Church, Millennials, and Religion*, vol. 1, *Prospects and Problems* (Eugene, OR: Cascade Books, 2018).

[6] See for instance, Tony Jones, "Is Emergent the New Christian Left? Tony Jones Responds to the Critics," *Christianity Today*, May 23, 2006, https://www.christianitytoday.com/pastors/2006/may-online-only/is-emergent-new-christian-left-tony-jones-responds-to.html and Brian D. McLaren, "The Politics of Joy," *Sojourners: God's Politics* (blog), December 15, 2006, sojo.net/articles/brian-mclaren-politics-joy.

[7] Cf. Mario L. Small, Robert A. Manduca, and William R. Johnston, "Ethnography, Neighborhood Effects, and the Rising Heterogeneity of Poor Neighborhoods Across Cities," *City and Community* 17, no. 3 (September 2018): 565–89, http://dx.doi.org/10.1111/cico.12316.

congregations—and to a lesser degree, key leaders—especially a relatively small number of ideal type communities.[8] Unfortunately, *CBRF* reinforces this critique. Excluding Chapter 2 (Marti's summary of *The Deconstructed Church*), the six chapters of *CBRF* that employ fieldwork cover a total of twenty-one congregations, twelve of which are in Alvizo's Chapter 4.[9] In fact, the same three congregations were studied in more than one chapter of *CBRF*, reducing the number of unduplicated congregations across the whole volume to just eighteen.

Case studies and small samples are certainly justifiable for a given project, but as this volume unintentionally shows, most work about the ECM considers a small number of homogenous communities, creating a research tautology in the process. Scholars want to study the ECM, but because there has been little institutionalization, researchers are left to examine existing ECM literature to identify congregations for study, thus ending up with many of the same communities.[10] Future research on the ECM should not only explore other communities, but perhaps more importantly, it should consider alternative units of analysis, such as individuals, organizations, gatherings, and quasi-institutional campaigns.[11] Other units should include seminaries, denominations, and judicatories, as well as overall society itself, at least insofar as the ECM has had some impact on broader cultural, religious, and societal institutions.[12] Given how elusive the ECM has been for researchers, future work might also consider innovative methodologies, such as network analysis and other indirect ways of measuring the ECM's cultural diffusion. Perhaps the ECM—in its own way—will bring out the most creative methodological and analytical impulses of future scholars.

The relatively small universe of congregational research subjects within ECM scholarship raises a final point, namely the challenge of quantifying the impact and significance of the movement, something with which scholarship about the ECM has long wrestled. As Packard notes in the Forward to *CBRF*, they are still open questions as to how wide the impact of the ECM really is or how lasting it will be, queries that *CBRF* does not directly attempt to answer. Ten or fifteen years ago, when scholars first began studying the ECM, the future of the movement was very much undetermined, but expectations were high that a generational change was underway in which "Emerging Christian" might soon be an identifiable and viable religious identity.[13] Would the ECM mirror Methodism, which began as a non-sectarian, grassroots revival movement and within sixty years had institutionalized to become one of the largest

---

[8] Ideal type is a concept attributed to sociologist Max Weber that refers to the creation of a mental or theoretical construct possessing all the essential properties of the entity under consideration with the understanding that such constructs serve analytical purposes and do not exist in the real world. Cf. Rolf E. Rogers, *Max Weber's Ideal Type Theory* (New York: Philosophical Library, Inc., 1969).

[9] Marti's book, *The Deconstructed Church*, is based upon participant observations at six different Emerging congregations, supplemented with materials from other individuals, events, and congregations.

[10] There are exceptions to this ethnographic, congregational focus, such as two pieces by Ryan P. Burge and Paul A. Djupe, "Emergent Church Practices in America: Inclusion and Deliberation in American Congregations," *Review of Religious Research* 57, no. 1 (2015): 1–23, http://dx.doi.org/10.1007/s13644-014-0157-2 and "An Emergent Threat: Christian Clergy Perceptions of the Emerging Church Movement," *Journal for the Scientific Study of Religion* 56, no. 1 (2017): 26–32, https://doi.org/10.1111/jssr.12324.

[11] See the socio-psychological and philosophical analysis by Darren M. Slade, "The Logic of Intersubjectivity: Brian McLaren's Philosophy of Christian Religion" (PhD diss., Liberty University, 2019).

[12] For example, one paradox that persists within the ECM—and which could be studied at the institutional level—is how the ECM is at once a reaction to conservative evangelicalism while also being intertwined and even dependent upon mainline Protestantism. There is debate as to whether the ECM has been assimilated into mainline Protestantism or remains a challenge to evangelicalism, which seems like fertile ground for future scholarly research.

[13] Bielo, *Emerging Evangelicals*, 26.

denominations in America?[14] Or would the ECM be like evangelicalism, a cross-denominational identifier that represents adherence to certain core theological affirmations (and later, political ones)? Or would it be like most new religious movements, which do not survive? Over a decade on, it is still challenging to know what to make of the ECM. Although some declared the movement dead long ago, new books and articles about the ECM continue to be written. Clawson and Stace, for their part, name the ECM an "important phenomenon within twenty-first century religion" (11). Perhaps the foremost call to future scholars of the ECM is to interrogate and then quantify this claim. The fruits of such an inquiry can comprise the next volume of scholarship about the ECM another decade from now; until then, *CBRF* will serve as the best single source of ECM scholarship to date.

BIBLIOGRAPHY

Bainbridge, William Sims. *The Sociology of Religious Movements*. New York: Routledge, 1997.

Bielo, James S. *Emerging Evangelicals: Faith, Modernity, and the Desire for Authenticity*. New York: NYU Press, 2011. https://doi.org/10.18574/nyu/9780814789544.001.0001.

Burge, Ryan P., and Paul A. Djupe. "Emergent Church Practices in America: Inclusion and Deliberation in American Congregations." *Review of Religious Research* 57, no. 1 (2015): 1–23. http://dx.doi.org/10.1007/s13644-014-0157-2.

———. "An Emergent Threat: Christian Clergy Perceptions of the Emerging Church Movement." *Journal for the Scientific Study of Religion* 56, no. 1 (2017): 26–32, https://doi.org/10.1111/jssr.12324.

Chia, Lloyd. "Emerging Faith Boundaries: Bridge-Building, Inclusion, and the Emerging Church Movement in America." PhD diss., University of Missouri-Columbia, 2010. https://mospace.umsystem.edu/xmlui/bitstream/handle/10355/10278/research.pdf?sequence=3.

Fitch, David. "Why the Missional/Emerging Church is so Young and White." *Missio Alliance* (blog), January 16, 2009. https://www.missioalliance.org/why-the-missionalemerging-church-is-so-young-and-white/.

Guest, Mathew. "The Emerging Church in Transatlantic Perspective." *Journal for the Scientific Study of Religion* 56, no. 1 (March 2017): 41–51. https://doi.org/10.1111/jssr.12326.

Jones, Tony. "How White Is the Emerging Church?." *Theoblogy*, May 8, 2012. https://www.patheos.com/blogs/tonyjones/2012/05/08/how-white-is-the-emerging-church/.

———. "Is Emergent the New Christian Left? Tony Jones Responds to the Critics." *Christianity Today*, May 23, 2006. https://www.christianitytoday.com/pastors/2006/may-online-only/is-emergent-new-christian-left-tony-jones-responds-to.html.

Marti, Gerardo, and Gladys Ganiel. *The Deconstructed Church: Understanding Emerging Christianity*. New York: Oxford University Press, 2014. https://doi.org/10.1093/acprof:oso/9780199959884.001.0001.

McLaren, Brian D. "The Politics of Joy." *Sojourners: God's Politics* (blog), December 15, 2006. https://sojo.net/articles/brian-mclaren-politics-joy.

Packard, Josh. *The Emerging Church: Religion at the Margins*. Religion in Politics and Society. Boulder, CO: First Forum Press, 2012.

---

[14] For the trajectory of Methodism, see William Sims Bainbridge, *The Sociology of Religious Movements* (New York: Routledge, 1997), 71–72.

Rah, Soong-Chan, and Jason Mach. "Is the Emerging Church for Whites Only?" *Sojourners Magazine*, May 2010.

Reed, Randall, and G. Michael Zbaraschuk. *The Emerging Church, Millennials, and Religion*. Vol. 1, *Prospects and Problems*. Eugene, OR: Cascade Books, 2018.

Rogers, Rolf E. *Max Weber's Ideal Type Theory*. New York: Philosophical Library, Inc., 1969.

Slade, Darren M. "The Logic of Intersubjectivity: Brian McLaren's Philosophy of Christian Religion." PhD diss., Liberty University, 2019.

Small, Mario L., Robert A. Manduca, and William R. Johnston. "Ethnography, Neighborhood Effects, and the Rising Heterogeneity of Poor Neighborhoods Across Cities." *City and Community* 17, no. 3 (September 2018): 565–89. http://dx.doi.org/10.1111/cico.12316.

ABOUT THE AUTHOR

Robert D. Francis is a doctoral candidate in Sociology at Johns Hopkins University. His research interests include work and occupations, social class, and rural communities. Bob conducted original research about the Emerging Church Movement in 2005–2006 as a master's student at the University of Chicago. Beginning in the Fall of 2019, Bob will be an Assistant Professor of Sociology at Whitworth University in Spokane, Washington.

MORE FROM THE AUTHOR

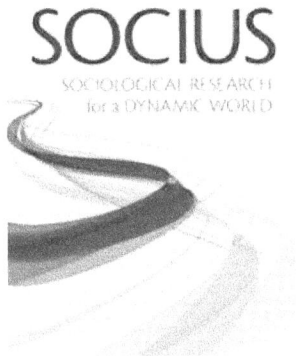

"Fatherhood in a Changing Economy,"
Public Justice Review 4, no. 4 (2017),
cpjustice.org/uploads/Fatherhood_in_a_Ch
anging_Economy_(PJR_Vol_4_No_4).pdf.

Robert D. Francis

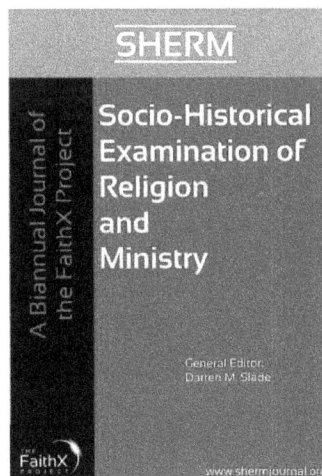

**"Him, Not Her: Why Working-class White
Men Reluctant about Trump Still Made
Him President of the United States,"**
*Socius: Sociological Research
for a Dynamic World* 4 (2018): 1-11,
http://dx.doi.org/10.1177/2378023117736486

Robert D. Francis

www.ingramcontent.com/pod-product-compliance
Lightning Source LLC
Chambersburg PA
CBHW081420270326
41931CB00015B/3351